# The Last Amendment

T. A. Miller

ISBN: 1537208683
ISBN-13: 978-1537208688

To Nicole, for our Jessie

# PROLOGUE

June 16, 2024

It is dawn on the day of Expiration. I am writing from a bench along Albert Street in the city of Martinsburg. The sky is clear, the air cool and dry. It is already a beautiful day and quite a few are walking to church. Most people smile at me, some wish me good morning, and a few, the wise, look at this journal with wonder. To write on paper, a miracle.

I will not go on to Sharpsburg with the rest. I do not have the heart to see the ceremony at noon. I have come far and am now so close but Grandpa did not live to see this, what he started. This is my second entry since his death, and the first since he was buried. I have written countless words but never until now, this moment, longed to hear the actual sound of my pencil writing them, the scratch against the page, the birth wail of meaning. It is because he is gone. Grandpa was my ears and he is gone.

I am grateful to Dr. Braddock for saving the letters Grandpa wrote him, and for giving them to me. And I am grateful for the letters Grandpa left at his bedside, two stacks, mine and Dr. Braddock's, each held neatly in place with three river stones. It seems this diary, my letters to and from Grandpa, and Grandpa's letters to and from Dr.

Braddock all tell a story, the story of the end of a nation, and the genesis of two new nations in its place. And these ribbons of words tell Grandpa's story. They tell mine. One day I shall order this diary and these letters into a book. Then I shall leave it somewhere, somewhere sacred, somewhere the world can find it once I have gone.

# 1

November 6, 2008

Dear Bart:

Thank you for the congratulatory message – I apologize for not answering your call last night. Following my opponent's concession, Beth rightly insisted I disregard the phone and focus solely on our honored houseguests. Family, friends, and many good people of Virginia kept us joyfully occupied well into the wee hours. While listening to your message this morning I laughed heartily at the indifference in your voice. I suppose fifteen reelections impart a certain levelheadedness with respect to the process. As this was my first, however, I shall require your tolerance of any lingering euphoria I may exhibit.

Ruth shared with Beth your intent to retrieve your nephew from Washington & Lee after the semester ends in mid-December. Please plan on lodging with us. You know Lexington is beautiful at Christmastime and the girls love a full house. In fact, they have already drawn up an itinerary for your stay. There is to be hot apple cider with cinnamon rolls at the lodge, then a horse-drawn carriage ride around the lake, then ice-skating and sledding in the park, and then board games back home in front of a roaring fire (with plenty of cocoa, of course). Should it snow, trust

Beth will insist upon a winding stroll through campus. It is simply glorious when frosted.

You have consistently rebuffed my gestures of gratitude for your generous counsel and honest friendship these past two years. Grant me, then, this one thing — the great privilege of welcoming you and Ruth into our home.

Yours sincerely,

Geoff

P.S. Your granddaughter Bee remains in our prayers. I know how much she means to you, and you to her. We have mentioned her struggle with sustained fever to various doctor friends. Regrettably, none has offered novel perspective, though all have acknowledged hearing loss as a potential side effect.

# 2

December 24, 2008

Dear Diary:

You are a gift from Grandpa. He told me I could open you early because you will help me get better. He said I should write in you every day. I cannot hear anything now. I cannot hear the dogs bark or the gun. I cannot hear Mother's tea pot. I can see everyone is worried about me. I do not miss the sounds but I do miss the voices. I cannot hear Father when he prays with me at bedtime. I remember the things he says. I do not know if he still says them. Now Father prays with his eyes closed tight. He squeezes my hands. Before Father prayed to pray with me. Now he means what he is praying. I think that is good. Before Mother hugged me to feel love. Now she hugs me to tell me she loves me. The boys are different around me. They act like they will break me if they move fast or laugh. That makes me very lonely. It makes me feel like I am not real anymore. Grandma tells me I will hear again soon. She says I will wake up one morning and hear again like before. I do not believe it. I think she says it so much to help her believe it. Grandpa is the same to me. He is the same in every way. He talks to me the same. He moves the same. His face is the same. This makes me so happy. If Grandpa is not sad about me I am not sad about me. There are many presents for me under the tree but I already know you are my favorite.

# 3

May 11, 2010

Happy 11<sup>th</sup> birthday, Bee. I wonder how long it'll take you to discover this letter. Not long, I suppose. In fact, I'll bet you climb up here and find it by the end of the day. Are you smiling now as you imagine your grumpy old grandfather struggling his way up a swaying and twisting rope ladder? I hope so because that smile of yours is a marvelous thing.

I saw it, you know, during Jonathan's band concert this morning – your smile. It didn't reveal itself because of the music, of course. That wouldn't do the trick. I think it couldn't help appearing when you saw the great ridiculous strain on your poor brother's face as he blew into that trumpet. I think you sensed how truly awful he and his band mates sounded and that made his desperate expression all the funnier. You didn't see me watching you, but I sure was. And I was smiling at your smiling.

Out on the trail this afternoon you asked me what you sound like when you speak. I could tell it was the first time you've asked anyone that question. Perhaps it's been long enough now and so you've forgotten. I didn't answer you on the trail but I'll answer you now. Every once and a while God forgets to close the door to heaven and angels sneak glances down to earth. When they see faces of babies and snowy mountains and little ducklings and ocean waves and deer running through the woods, the angels whisper to each other joyfully. That's what you sound like when you speak – like one of those whispering angels.

You are the Songbird, Bee. Please don't stop singing.

Loving you forever,

Grandpa

# 4

January 23, 2012

Diary:

I am writing from the glen. This morning I went to leave early but Mother was waiting. She begged me not to go. I told her that I must. Father and the rest of the boys were still sleeping but Peter had woken with the dawn. He came and stood by my side. He said to Mother in a very loving way "Please let her go. Her journey has great meaning for her." I believe he knows of my suffering. I brought Mary with me. She was happy to finally come outside but she struggled walking because of thick ice atop the snow. I could feel it crunching and breaking beneath her feet. It must have been loud even a long way away. When I arrived the glen looked like it had been turned to crystal. The sun came out from behind the clouds and everything sparkled. It was the most beautiful sight I have ever seen. Now the clouds are back and strong wind is swirling them around the sky. It looks like milk going into tea. The air is so cold but I am not. It is wonderful here in my secret place. I am at peace. Today is a good day.

# 5

October 31, 2017

Peter woke me last night. All the lights were on! It has been so long. Tomorrow will be eleven months since the attacks. Mother sat crying by the fire. I saw Father looking at me with tears in his eyes. This made me cry. He smiled and said not to tell the boys. I laughed and cried more. In such times it must be difficult being a father to a daughter. It soon went dark again but I did not stop crying for joy. Father found me and held me close until I fell asleep. I woke up this morning beneath the white wool blanket.

After breakfast I almost did not get away. Mother said it was not safe because of the drifters. She said chickens and hogs are being stolen. But Father said "Let her go. She is a smart girl and Mary will be with her." I did not see any deer in the woods but some must still live there. I found depressions in the long grass not covered in dew. Twice I smelled upturned soil and noticed scars in the leaves where hooves had been raking. I am grateful for these signs.

Mother made a wonderful lunch of stew from squirrel and vegetables from the cellar. She used the last of the wheat flour for rolls. I think she wished to celebrate the promise of last night's lights. The boys still make me eat first. I hate it. I know it is because they love me. But I hate it because I love them too. They ate so much more before. They are always hungry now. In this world it must be difficult being a brother to a sister. I love them so much. I hope they know it. I tell them but they just act like boys when I do. I hope they truly know how much I love them.

Now I am writing from the wagon. We are headed to Grimm's Landing to register. Father wonders if this might be the last time. He says it can now be proven that nothing was done to the water. They simply lied to frighten those without a well. What an evil that is. If electricity returns, people will be able to start communicating again. The afternoon is sunny and cool. There are no clouds at all. Most trees have lost leaves, but not the oaks. The oaks hold onto their leaves. I wonder if it is out of loyalty or stubbornness.

Mary is angry with Peter. It is because in guiding her he has too much heart and not enough patience. Grandma is reading Grandpa's letter aloud for the third time. I do not find it as funny as the boys since he says he is a prisoner in the depths of hell. There must be truth in that. He is strong but he is tired. He has told me so. I miss him dearly. Mother is sorting her herbs. She is very proud of them. I can sense that Father is tempted to say they will not fetch much at trade so I am sitting between him and Mother. I may have to remind him of his promise.

# 6

November 25, 2017

Dear Bart:

You are a most observant friend, and a shrewd friend at that. Last night you sensed my intensifying battle with gloom and confronted the demon head-on by asking what I remember of that day, now almost one year past. You countered my mute despondency by directing me to think about the question and write down my answer. You know well that writing soothes me, that it helps me clarify my thoughts and, therefore, order and bracket my fears. Simply contemplating this letter over breakfast this morning has yielded a curative effect. The great blessing of older, wiser, assertively honest friends dawns on me anew. Thank you.

I remember the morning routine beginning as usual, as it was for all of us beyond earshot of the night's explosions. But whether by television, computer, or phone, there soon came connection with the outside world. It had to have been a collective gaping-mouth stupor unrivaled in human history, as three hundred million Americans discovered their lifeblood being devoured by flame and hemorrhaging into oceans, and then their realization that any ability to refine black gold had been crippled by the detonation of thirty refineries. Ah, our addiction, our withdrawal…

I remember work commutes and school treks being abandoned. The wise dashed for cash, gas, and groceries while the spellbound masses took up vigil in front of digital screens. Closings and cancellations scrolled beneath the featherweights manning the morning's wake-up shows. They played their parts the only way they knew how, continually reiterating the obvious while vetting wild speculations. Just before noon came the water rumor, that allegation that most of America's fresh water supplies had been tainted overnight with a highly potent, incredibly lethal neurotoxin. Detailed maps, photographs, time-lines, and illustrations emerged showing how the poison had been strategically distributed into lakes, streams, and tributaries across the fruited plain.

The water rumor was a very useful ruse. Americans not already dreading inadequately stocked pantries suddenly were. Panic drove millions to search for bottled drinks, canned and boxed food, medicine, ammunition, batteries, and all other staples of life. Torrents of frantic shoppers clogged roadways and choked parking lots. The desperate scramble for what were now known to be finite resources was an effective distraction for civilians and an unshakable diversion for law enforcement officials all afternoon. Unnoticed amidst the bedlam, then, went those hundreds of windowless work vans, each painted and tagged convincingly to match the fleet of the local power company. Drivers had probably lain in wait all morning, each in proximity to his designated high-voltage power transmission substation. With the chaos of the water rumor in full effect, drivers closed on their prey, cruising down service roads, and compromising chain-link fences without anyone watching.

As the late afternoon sun nosed into the horizon, palpable worry turned to guttural desperation. Hoarding had cleared shelves and emptied fuel supplies. The sudden prospect of long-term scarcity without relief disintegrated civic decency and diluted social order. At approximately 4 p.m. came the first declarations of martial law. By sunset, a faint but genuine whiff of anarchy could be detected. Just after 6 p.m., with the last vestiges of red, orange, and purple fleeing the western sky, the substations exploded. Power-surges whistled through the network, destroying infrastructure as they went. In less than sixty seconds the nation's power grid collapsed.

It was done this way on purpose, of course, the impenetrable darkness coming last. It had been important to observe everything choreographed. It had been important for our terror to well while the lights were on. We had been allowed to witness the beast arriving in our doorway. We had been allowed to see him pause there in the threshold. And we had been allowed to watch him take that first step toward us before the lights went out. Now, in the season of longest nights, our furnace motors would not whirl, pushing their warm air. Our appliances would be lifeless, useless, unable to clean or dry clothes, wash dishes, refrigerate, bake, fry, or sauté food. Water would not be pumped, and only by fire could it be boiled. Anew, flame would be appreciated – cherished – because it would be needed, our only option for cooking, heating, sterilizing, and illuminating. Communication would devolve. Nothing but vocal cords, ear drums, and eyeballs would matter once the batteries died. Our once great contiguous continent would be forced through a screen, sifted into a million islands. Nothing would be certain outside the home, through the front door, down the steps, into the frontier.

I cannot help admitting, it was a perfect work.

Geoff

# 7

February 15, 2018

Bee, your questions are so wise, so far beyond your years. Such questions are the product of stillness, silence, and solitude. You were forced into the silence and you often choose the stillness and the solitude. It's only natural, then, for such questions to take root. The extraordinary darkness of our times is causing the questions to haunt you.

Over the years I've shared with your brothers many stories of my time in Vietnam. The boys are excited by risky adventure and so drawn to it, as I was at their age. But I've never shared with them, or with anyone, not even Grandma, the worst of my stories. Those things I keep locked deeply in my mind because no good can come from letting them out. Those things must die along with me someday. Usually those things are asleep or maybe hibernating. Every now and then, though, they wake. When I was a younger man, their anger meant my anger, their horror meant my horror, and their sadness meant my sadness. As I aged, I discovered a medicine. Stillness, silence, and solitude calm those things. Stillness, silence, and solitude put them back to sleep. But stillness, silence, and solitude produce the same side effect in Bartholomew Scattercorn as they do in his granddaughter. They conjure those questions of purpose and destiny that cause the two of us to wonder so deeply.

Is life just a riddle to solve? Are its twists simply the doors of a damn puzzle box, or the turns in a maze? Do we get to leave only if the dots get connected correctly, or if we find the X on the map? Or is life some kind of test or examination? If so, then to what standard, and where is the proctor? Or maybe life's some sort of worthiness challenge? But then for what reward, and to which consequence? Maybe life is a grand science experiment? An opportunity for the maker to observe what happens to reactants when the temperature is raised or the pressure increased? Or perhaps it's nothing more than an endurance challenge. Just make it a certain distance and you win...

My wonderings on these things are grounded by an experience I had over fifty years ago. This Grandma knows, but no one else. I share it with you, Bee, because I believe you are the meaning. At the end of a long day's march, my company was led up King's Mountain in North Carolina. It was the middle of August and hot as hell. Several men had already dropped from heat stroke or dehydration. When we reached the summit, everyone shed his gear and spread out to rest. Most reclined on the sloping rock to enjoy the view, some went and lay in the shade of the trees, but I was very lightheaded and had bad cramps in both legs so I kept moving. I ended up on this impressive outcropping. It was a nifty spot and I remember being surprised that no one else had found the place. I sat down and closed my eyes to see if that'd make the lightheadedness go away. I don't honestly know how long my eyes were closed, maybe a minute, maybe five, but I remember opening them to the sound of hard-soled shoes on rock. I saw a funny little man walking toward me. He was short, bowlegged, and moved with a teetering wobble, like a duck. He was very old and dressed fancily, but his suit jacket and pants were far too large for him. He wore thick glasses and had an overgrown moustache. He smiled very warmly at me and I smiled back. There was something amazingly charming about the old man, a beloved uncle sort of quality. He came right up to me and said without hesitation, "Hello, Bart." I asked him how he knew my name. He said, "Oh I know everything about you." Then I remember closing my eyes tightly and counting slowly to five. I opened my eyes and he was still there. He said, "I'm still here!" and he laughed. I think I laughed too. Then I asked him if he was an angel. The funny little man smiled and said, "No, but boy will they find that funny!" And that's how I knew who he was. I remember closing my eyes again, this time because they were stinging. When I opened them he was still there smiling at me. I asked him "What is the purpose of my life?" For the first time the smile left his face, though he still looked kind. He peered over my shoulder into the distance and said, "To be a block in the arch."

I can't remember at all descending the mountain or driving

back to the base, and none of my friends had seen the funny little man that day. I might have been hallucinating. That's what Grandma thinks. Regardless, his answer to my last question remains with me. If I am after all nothing more or less than a block in the arch, then you, Bee, must be its keystone. I pray that while your life fire burns the hottest and shines the brightest, you will see, feel, taste, touch, and even hear the purpose of your life, and then live it out completely. This world will be the better for it.

Love,

Grandpa

# 8

December 17, 2018

Geoff, here's my farewell speech. I know you have Beth and the girls in town with you so don't fret not getting to this before I go on. I wouldn't change anything even if you told me to. Giving it to you is for posterity – you're the historian. After tonight I'm off to peace and seclusion. It's been a pleasure working with you. You know I'm no bullshitter so trust when I say you're as noble a man as I've ever known. If the heathens in this place appreciated a person's goodness like I do they'd have long ago made you Speaker. Here, at the parting, know you've earned in abundance that one thing I reserve most jealously – my respect. Bart

Tonight, Mr. Speaker, I conclude my fortieth year as a member of this body. My friends and family know I don't waste words and tonight will be no different. In a moment I'll walk out those doors for the last time and journey back to Apple Grove, West Virginia, the place I've proudly called home for every one of my seventy two years. I was born and grew up there, got married there, raised my family there, and buried my wife there. My children live there, and their children. I wish to die there and be buried next to Ruth. Whenever God wants me, I am ready. I give thanks to the voters who elected me those twenty times. I have never failed to appreciate the honor of representing them. I also thank those who didn't vote for me those twenty times and yet respected the process enough to let me represent them anyway.

I have seen and learned much during my years as a United States Congressman. I hope I have affected some things for the better, and helped defeat some things of the worse. But nothing in my time here compares in either magnitude or power to the economic nightmare in which we find ourselves. No war, no attack, no natural disaster, no assassination, nothing, nothing in these many years compares. Despair and hopelessness have this nation by the throat and will not let go. You may call me a coward for walking away now, in the midst of all this, and perhaps you're right to do so. But I am an old man and have neither the vitality nor the will left to battle on. I do have the strength, though, to leave you one last something, an idea, my parting gift.

For eighty years conservatives have known they were hoodwinked by FDR and his New Deal. They were sold that it would save America from that first Great Depression, and so they bought in. But conservatives never could've dreamed the bureaucratic monsters they were helping spawn, creatures that would grow to be self-sustaining, self-preserving, and insatiable, bent on gobbling up more and more of our economy with each passing year. Yes, that's right, conservatives stood by and watched, enabled even, the establishment of a permanent entitlement culture and its supportive infrastructures. Well today's conservatives haven't forgotten their ancestors' selling out and bankrupting of principles. And so today's conservatives are refusing to let it happen again, refusing to grant extraordinary powers or latitudes of any kind to this government for any reason whatsoever, regardless how badly those powers and those latitudes may be needed, regardless how much relief they might bring those in great suffering.

For just as long, liberals have been told to trust the free market, to let it run and frolic about unabated. They've been told that uninhibited, unrestricted, unregulated capitalism is the most effective cure to any of humanity's problems. Well the liberals know they too have been hoodwinked. Through the years they've been coerced into pampering whole industries and entire segments of the economy, granting no-strings-attached licenses to earn profits without any obligations to pay dividends to the communities and peoples and cultures which enabled the profiteers to harvest their returns. Yes, liberals know that free markets can innovate and solve problems, but they've seen those free markets all too often betray humanity for a marginally better return on equity. And so liberals are refusing to entrust the nation's salvation in any way to the soulless parasites of industry, no matter how badly their remedies might be needed.

This government is mortally gridlocked while the nation strangles. The President hasn't been presented with a bill to sign in six months because the Senate is exactly tied, constantly filibustered, paralyzed, and impotent. The opposition party controls this body, so no help for the President here. Bills that do pass and survive Senate filibusters are vetoed. Overrides fail. The President writes executive orders, we withhold funds and issue floods of subpoenas. The House impeaches, the Senate doesn't convict. Circuit courts overrule to scorn and the Supreme Court remands to spite. We are impossibly quagmired, stuck in an absolute ideological stalemate, perfectly and seemingly permanently gridlocked. And the nation strangles. It strangles.

My daddy died in World War II. He only ever held me in his arms once, when I was first born. Then he went off and died somewhere in the fields of France, fighting the Nazis. I never knew my daddy. I grew up without the love of a daddy because he went and died for freedom. He didn't die for this. He died for freedom. My daddy died for freedom.

Freedom. It is freedom that was died for. And so it is freedom that must survive. This, this infernal hell we've created for ourselves, it should be put to rest, mercy-slain once and for all. Split the country in half and create two new nations. Give the conservatives the red states. Give the liberals the blue states. Let's just formalize what we've been drifting toward for decades. In this way each ideology can solve its problems exactly the way it wants to, exactly the way it needs to. We've failed freedom by living as one. Now we must ensure she lives by cutting her out of her dead mother. To keep freedom alive, and to let her thrive once again, we must bury The United States of America. May Holy God and the million patriots forgive me for saying so.

# 9

January 5, 2019

Dear Grandpa:

I am sorry you did not come to New Year's. I know that you miss Grandma and it is too difficult for you to be around everyone. I saw it in your eyes at Christmas. You should not stay so alone out there in the woods. I know you wish to heal on your own but it is not good for a sad heart to be a lonely one. I must leave for school early tomorrow but I will ride out to see you my first weekend back. I promise.

Do you realize what your goodbye speech is doing? Your idea has excited everyone. It is all over the news. They are asking if you meant to do this, if you had any idea what you were starting. I think back to the time you and Peter set the yard on fire. Mother and Grandma were so angry! I am laughing now thinking of you and Peter running to stomp out the fire while they shouted at you! You might have done it again, Grandpa. You might have started another fire.

Today it has been 10 years exactly. Do you remember? The doctor told us my hearing would not return. I learned that I would be deaf forever. Everyone cried, even Father and the boys. But not you and not me. I remember you looking at me with fire in your eyes. Then you came over to me and knelt down. I watched your mouth closely, thinking you would say something to me. But you did not. You very slowly tapped me three times above my heart. Then you pressed your finger to my lips and held it there for a second. And then you took my hands and squeezed them and held them. I remember feeling great comfort in what you did, even though I did not understand it. I still do not, and you have never told me. But while everyone around me cried in sadness, I felt peace and even hope.

I wish I could make you feel that same peace and hope, Grandpa. I love you more than words can express.

Bee

# 10

January 25, 2019

Dear Bart:

I pray the first month of your retirement has proven genuinely liberating and breathed new life into your soul. The thought of you roaming snowy hillsides on horseback makes me smile, as does the image of you porch-rocking while wrapped in your bear fur and drawing from that filthy old pipe. My friend, I hope you have found joyful, abiding rest in the shadows of the woods. Beth sends you her selfless love. I send you my selfish regret, for I miss seeing you every day.

I further pray this letter reaches you at all. The Postmaster still lists service in your region as intermittent so, certain as I am you will continue avoiding all forms of electronic communication regardless how benignly convenient they may be, I have little choice but to employ ink, paper, and stamp to solicit your wisdom. Perhaps this has been your plan all along. If so, I commend you, for your solitude seems secure.

Your family have undoubtedly shared that the punch line to your farewell address has struck a chord. Whether or not you actually intended to ignite a revolution, you have become cult pontiff over the concept of bisecting the nation by ideology. Given the closeness and longevity of our friendship, as well as the perceived permanency of your seclusion, I have been named emissary to you – my charge, to solicit your input into this matter. It is naturally presumed that your endorsements (even implicit) as to the various ways and means of the movement will give credence to the whole.

Your disciples' first challenge was determining how to actually execute a purposeful, permanent bisection of the United States. Proposals were wide-ranging and hotly debated, but all seemed impractical in at least a few meaningful aspects. Against all better judgment I stepped forward and suggested the United States could be effectively extinguished by employing a constitutional amendment. I argued this might allow a careful, methodical winding down of the government while simultaneously enabling the reordering of American society into two ideologically-opposite offspring nations. The proposal has taken root. Key tenets of my rationalization follow. I most expectantly await your thoughts and suggestions.

Although the Constitution stipulates governmental structure and procedures, articulates forbiddances and limitations of powers, consecrates human rights, and enshrines civic privileges, the document lists no provision for its own nullification as the nation's underlying and preeminent legal framework. In other words, the Constitution is completely silent with respect to its own mortality. An amendment executed a) in strict accordance with the Constitution's explicit instructions and b) consistent with the historical cadence (i.e. rhythm and lingo) of prior successful amendments seems the optimal platform for governing the termination of the document as a whole.

The Constitution's authors considered its malleability to be an essential attribute. The evolution of American society has periodically required further clarification or greater potency from the document, e.g. voting age, privacy rights, income tax, minority rights, assault rifles, abortion, etc. As you know, the founders afforded us two methods by which to 'edit' the Constitution's text and, hence, change the meaning and authority of the document: 1) interpretation of its wording by the Judicial Branch, enabled by Article III then enforced in practice by stare decisis, and 2) the amendment process offered in Article V.

Regarding Judicial Interpretation – as I note above, the Constitution is devoid of instructions on how it might be terminated in its entirety. Suppose that pro-bisection states were to sue the federal government with the aim of securing a mass release from the auspices of the Constitution. Inevitably the Supreme Court would hear and rule on the case. For the states to triumph, the court would have to find that their withdrawal from the authority of the Constitution is somehow, ironically, constitutional. If so, any and all of the fifty states would then be permitted to re-aggregate themselves into new nations as they see fit.

Even if this route were feasible, it would be fraught with peril. The entire bisection process – its goals, ways, and means – would very likely end up a corrupted, deformed child of the American judicial establishment. The nearly unimaginable complexity of designing and launching two completely new, ideologically opposite 21$^{st}$ Century nations would be beholden to the random discretion of nine judges, all of whom reap their fame, fortune, and earthly purpose from the bureaucracy they would be working to extinguish. This notion is beyond extraordinary. It is ludicrous.

So it is the amendment process of Article V that I favor. Regarding…

Pathway – The amendment process can be initiated and administered completely independent of the Congress, the president, and the federal judiciary via a convention of the states. None of the previous twenty eight amendments have been passed in this manner but this pathway is free (hypothetically) of federal obstacles. Obviously, the Washington bureaucracy and ruling political class of each party are not enthusiastic about facilitating their own extinction. Steering clear of them, therefore, is prudent.

Clarity – Unlike a law, an amendment is inordinately more difficult to dilute or contaminate through Congressional or Executive tinkering. If authored wisely, an amendment's substance, mechanisms, and potency cannot be readily altered, thereby helping ensure the states' their right to choose the gender, eye color, and so on of their fraternal twin babies.

Fairness – The amendment route is inherently, conspicuously democratic in nature. It is the ultimate populist tool, the purest manifestation of the Will of the People. This makes the approach easily marketable, especially given the ever-quickening support for bisection.

Legitimacy – Internationally, to the community of nations, the amendment approach seems most likely to be respected and trusted. The U.S. Constitution has been the quintessential moral authority for self-rule for well over two centuries. An amendment to bring about bisection is the least coup-like option available. There is nothing revolutionary about Americans amending their Constitution, even to bring about this, albeit earth-shaking, change.

And so here is our first iteration. Appreciate, please, what is explicitly articulated, and what is deliberately not.

# Draft Amendment to expire the Constitution

*The Constitution of the United States of America and all authority therein shall expire on the third anniversary of the ratification of this amendment, at which time all elements of the government of the United States of America shall be assumed by the several states.*

*No later than one year from the ratification of this amendment, all the several states shall have aligned themselves by signed treaty or pact into two distinct confederations, else this amendment is repealed.*

*No later than two years from the ratification of this amendment, each of the two distinct confederations of states shall have established a democratic form of government for its own self-rule. Else, this amendment is repealed.*

Glad for your quick reply,

Yours gratefully,

Geoff

# 11

February 10, 2019

Geoff:

I was happy to find your letter in my mailbox. No, I do not intend to let electronics corrupt my seclusion. I'm glad you understand this. My typing this letter on a computer is the closest I'll come to relenting. You know me well because I've done little but ride and rock and smoke these past two months. My offspring have left me alone, as I asked. They know I need some time. There are no friends to bother me. The few men I called good friends are all dead now. I have no interest in new ones. There is peace in having dead good friends. There's no peace in trying to find new living ones. Only Bee has the courage to visit me. She knows I cannot refuse her. She is my songbird. I should say you are my good friend, Geoff. Maybe more like a son. I'm glad you wrote me.

I'm aware of the bisection movement. When I ride into town for groceries, shopkeeper Jay tells me news. He's careful because he knows I have little patience for it, but he's seen me furrow my brow and smile and shake my head at certain things. Honestly, I'm surprised at the groundswell. My intent was to somehow dislodge the partisan clot, not reform the nation. But if momentum is building then perhaps there's merit in the idea. If you've become involved because you believe there's purpose and nobility in it, I commend you and will help you as best I can. If you're involved because you feel you must be out of loyalty to me, you're a fool and I insist you withdraw at once. This could very well become a cause big enough for martyrs.

I've spent a few days thinking about your amendment's first draft. You know I'm a fan of brevity, but in the first paragraph you need to articulate more. When you say "…at which time all elements of the government of the United States…" you're inviting the tinkering you wisely hope to avoid. Does "all elements" mean physical assets? Or processes? Rights? You're not a lawyer. I am, or used to be. Trust that we're tactile sons of bitches. The exact meaning of the phrase "all elements of the government" is vague and so encourages manhandling in the guise of clarification.

I appreciate and agree with the necessity of your second paragraph, but the very first sentence of the Constitution's Article I, Section 10 is patently contrary. "No State shall enter into any Treaty, Alliance, or Confederation…" Logic dictates that the amendment supersedes, but even non-lawyers have sense enough to see direct conflict. I wouldn't risk a duel with one of the Constitution's old bones. I'd explicitly repeal that Article I, Section 10 clause as part of your amendment.

Lengthen the time between the amendment's ratification and the Constitution's expiration. Three years is too few, especially given the unknown which lies beyond. Quell the wolves' impatience by pointing out a longer time span helps them sell the amendment by making it appear less threatening, less reactionary, and less forced.

Also in this light, you need an easy out, something offering Americans a reasonable opportunity to change their minds. This could be accomplished via another amendment, of course, but that's neither quick nor easy. Consider a circuit-breaker mechanism of some kind, something that provides a convenient ripcord. A national referendum comes to mind, where the citizens' direct vote could unwind bisection.

The biggest obstacle to your amendment's success is the question of what the hell comes after its ratification. How, exactly, do you transition from one nation into two? How do you do it in an orderly and peaceful fashion? Simply prescribing that all elements of a death-bound United States of America "be assumed by the several states" is insanity. Chaos will reign, regardless how well-meaning and apparently unified proponents of bisection seem. I suggest the amendment stipulate an independent agency be established to manage the details of bisection. Such an agency should be accountable only to the states and on their behalf: a) aggregate, organize, and coordinate bisection activities, b) shield the state governments from the many tactical distractions involved, and c) narrow and focus aspects of bisection *into a single apolitical entity outside the meddling powers of the federal government.

If this is a cause to which you truly ascribe, Geoff, then I'll help as best I can. Give Beth my love in return.

Bart

# 12

February 12, 2019

Today St. Paul's in Sanford. It sits so beautifully amongst the trees. There was a single car in the lot, beneath the bell tower. The old house next door must be the parsonage because the walk leading to it is plowed and salted. I knew the church would be unlocked. Pretty churches always are.

I stood in the unlit narthex for a while, looking into the nave. Long banks of windows up and down each side ushered in chalky daylight which highlighted rows of polished wood pews atop ruby red carpet. At the front, the altar area is very plain but neat, very simple and unadorned, but warm, even from a distance. The modest elegance drew me through the doors and down the aisle.

I had been at the altar for only a moment when a powerful sensation startled me. I felt vibrations deep inside. The hair on my neck stood up. I turned and saw light in the choir loft at the back of the church. A man was sitting at the organ console while two children ran around him. I wondered if the energy surging through me could be sound from the organ.

The children both saw me coming up the aisle. The little boy was very handsome, with striking eyes. The little girl was adorable, with curly blond hair and chubby cheeks. I paused just below the balcony and they both smiled at me through the railing. I felt the sound energy stop and an instant later the man appeared at the railing, looking down at me. I knew he must be their grandfather because the little girl grabbed onto his leg playfully. He grinned down at me in a closed mouth way and nodded slightly. It was a shy but welcoming expression. He said something but it was difficult to see his lips moving. I told him I was deaf. He smiled shyly again, with mouth closed, and nodded in an understanding way. Then he gestured for me to join them in the balcony. The little girl was now running back and forth along the rail, laughing. The little boy was staring at me with his striking eyes. I do not know why I was so drawn to go up to them but I did.

I felt the energy again as I climbed the stairs. When I reached the balcony the man was sitting at the console playing the keys. The little girl was sitting next to him on the bench. Up here the vibrations were so strong I could feel them in my bones. The handsome little boy greeted me and told me that his name was Andrew and that he was four years old. His lips were very easy to read and he spoke very slowly and clearly. He said his sister was almost two years old and that her name was Belle. I asked him if the man playing the organ was his grandfather and Andrew nodded and said the man's name was Pop Pop. He took my hand and walked me over to the organ console.

Pop Pop stopped playing and introduced himself as Edward. He had a very pleasant way about him. He asked about my deafness and was interested in how I could read lips. He explained all this to the children. Andrew seemed very curious. He touched his own ears while listening to his grandfather. But Belle seemed confused and maybe even a bit frightened. She pushed her face into Edward's side. He stood from the bench and picked up Belle in his arms and then asked me if I would like to see how the organ works. I said yes very much. Belle watched me closely with her face safely against her grandfather's chest. Andrew took my hand and led me toward the back wall of the choir loft. Edward unlocked a narrow door and Andrew pulled me forward into a dark space that smelled strongly of pine and faintly of wet paper.

When the light was turned on I was amazed. The room was filled with silver pipes of all sizes atop a giant wooden chest. From the chest came all sorts of cords and hoses. I noticed Edward watching me. He was enjoying my fascination. So was Belle, with her head still against his chest. Edward asked if I had ever seen a pipe organ up close before and I said no. Then Andrew squeezed my hand. I had forgotten he was holding it. I looked down and he was just smiling at me with his handsome smile. I smiled back at him and suddenly felt very warm and very glad to be with these people.

I turned to Edward and told him about the sound energy I

had felt earlier. I explained that I have been in churches with organs but had never felt that sensation. He laughed a little bit and said that I must not have ever been around a real pipe organ before. He explained that most churches these days have consoles that simply play the imitated sounds of pipes over electronic speakers. I asked why this organ would create that vibration energy inside me when all the others did not. He then showed me a pipe up close and the part called its mouth and described how wind is the pipe organ's secret. He said it is wind that gives the pipe organ power to penetrate the body and rattle the bones. He said it is wind that lets the pipe organ sing. Andrew let go of my hand and went over to a pipe with a narrow piece of red ribbon coming from its mouth. I saw him ask Edward why it was there. I turned in time to see Edward explain to Andrew that the pipe looks like all the others but it does not work. He told him that air flows through it but it makes no sound.

Belle squirmed so Edward set her down. She left the room quickly and Edward and Andrew followed her. Edward went and sat down on the console bench. Belle sat to his left and Andrew to his right. I said thank you and goodbye to all three of them. Andrew said something to me but I only saw his last three words – the holy ghost. Belle waved at me shyly. Edward smiled in his closed mouth way and nodded politely. Then he turned to his music and began playing and that energy filled me up. At the top of the stairs I turned back to enjoy the sight of them one last time. They were all looking forward, Edward at his hymnal and the children at his hands.

Correct in form, with wind rushing through me, but somehow and entirely broken. I am the pipe that does not sing.

# 13

March 10, 2019

Geoff:

Thank you for your regular and detailed updates. I appreciate it takes time and energy to write as you do. Very few put ink on paper anymore, let alone actual thought, let further alone deep thought. You and Bee are my only correspondents. I'm glad you both have the gift of expression and are each willing to share it with me.

It's clear you're reaching a crescendo with the amendment. Assuming my comments are still valuable to its disciples, take these to heart.

The treason concern is just rumor mongering bullshit from bisection opponents. I can't see it working effectively to derail the amendment. However, such sentiment might very well adversely affect the recruitment and retention of talent for the Section 2 agency. The post-ratification success of bisection will hinge on the effectiveness of that body. It needs to be staffed with top minds and leaders, not public-service flunkies. You'll never attract top minds and leaders to the agency if they sense employment there may imperil them. And you'll never retain them without a cleverly designed fringe benefits package, though that's a post-ratification issue which doesn't belong in the amendment itself. Point is – be boldly explicit with this matter. Make that last sentence of Section 2 more forceful by calling out the most egregious potential charges. "…deputies shall be forever immune from prosecution for Treason, Conspiracy, Espionage, or other high crimes against the United States…" Something like that.

In Section 3 I'm glad you addressed my post-ratification secession concern. I believe the potential withdrawal of even a single state from its chosen confederation was a reasonable vulnerability to the amendment's integrity, certainly in the eyes of the public and, more dangerously, in the eyes of the judiciary. That well-written sentence eliminates the risk entirely.

But my other significant concern with Section 3 remains. I again point out how establishing "confederations" (that word itself) is in direct conflict with Article I, Section 10 – not an amendment, mind you, but original body, founder-authored text. I appreciate that amendments do, both by definition and in practice, supersede earlier language in a legal document. And I also appreciate the Pandora's Box concerns over having to, then, explicitly repeal any and all other perceived conflicts between the amendment and earlier Constitutional text. The fact is, however, 600,000+ Civil War deaths resulted from a subset of states attempting to reaggregate themselves and split away from the rest. Americans once had it in their genetic makeup to slaughter each other over the essence of Article I, Section 10. I dare say that institutional memory remains. Though it appears a large majority now favor bisection, founders' words expressly forbidding it are like a bundle of very dry grass. We shouldn't leave an ember glowing. Repeal Article I, Section 10, or at least its first clause, as part of your amendment.

Finally, Section 6 needs to be deleted in its entirety. You indicate a groundswell toward pulling it out and I hope you do. "Neither the Congress nor the President nor the Supreme Court nor its inferior courts shall have power to affect this amendment." That's practically a dare for the bastards to come after it. Amendments have often granted Congress a license "to enforce this article by appropriate legislation" but a hands-off restriction, especially to all three branches of the government, is unprecedented. Besides being provocative, it's unnecessary. Pull it out.

Bart

# 14

March 28, 2019

Dear Bart:

Yesterday I enjoyed an impromptu lunch with the Chief Justice at Cosmo's. I know you will be glad to hear that old Cosmo's pizza remains as crunchy and delicious as his temper is foul (he berated me severely for daring to request a menu at the peak of the lunch rush). Mama's heartfelt, watery-eyed apologies, however, still elicit sympathetic tolerance from the unjustifiably abused clientele. Never in the history of business has a more dysfunctional value-proposition been so inexplicably sustained.

Especially noteworthy from my lunch encounter was the Chief Justice's casual willingness to discuss Bisection and, more importantly, how SCOTUS is likely to rule on appeal should the Seventh Circuit find against us. Recall the case seeking to enjoin all activities of amendment proponents on grounds their actions are unconstitutional. I pointed out to Mark that the range of speculation as to the Court's opinion on this matter is very broad because, with respect to it, he and his colleagues have remained virtually silent. I also told him plainly that some, especially those most conspicuously involved with the amendment process, are reasonably concerned about being arrested for Treason in light of the intensifying rumors to that effect. On both fronts Mark was forthright.

He explained that while under normal circumstances Supreme Court justices strenuously avoid hinting as to the Court's inclinations on an inbound case, they have, in fact, already done so with this one. At my great surprise, Mark smiled and offered that opponents of Bisection had very recently asked several justices point-blank their opinion of the amendment. He further offered that the several justices answered point-blank that amending the Constitution is and always has been a vital right of all Americans because (my paraphrasing) it allows them to change the rules when they no longer like the game, when the game no longer serves them. Mark then looked me in the eye and said meaningfully, "If you can't change the rules of the game, you're a slave."

When I wondered aloud why no word of the justices' sentiment had reached the media, Mark hypothesized it was likely because opponents of Bisection surmised the news would harm their marketing efforts. I then confessed my general surprise at the prospect of pro-Bisection like-mindedness amongst the justices, that we have been assuming ambivalence at best and more likely opposition from the courts. Mark pointed out plainly that there are few, if any, apolitical judges in the federal judiciary and so, as it is within the federal legislative and executive branches, the state governments, and the country at large, conservatives and liberals there are excited by the prospect of ridding themselves of each other. Ultimately, though Mark did not actually indicate how SCOTUS might rule on the Seventh Circuit's case, it seems clear SCOTUS justices are in strong, perhaps unanimous, agreement that pursuit of our amendment is lawful and legitimate.

Regarding concern over charges of Treason, Mark said any such anxiety is absolutely unwarranted. He said he cannot fathom any ideological judge (that's all of them) allowing an otherwise law-abiding American citizen to fester in a jail cell simply for organizing or having anything to do with an amendment to the Constitution. That said, he commended the immunity clause language added to Section 2 as a matter of cautious preemption, noting as you did its importance with respect to recruiting and retaining talent for the Agency.

The final draft will be ready shortly. I will send it as soon as possible. Though Section 3 does not contain the repeal (full or partial) of Article I, Section 10, that you so strongly suggested, I believe you will be otherwise pleased.

Yours sincerely,

Geoff

# 15

April 6, 2019

Dear Bart:

The draft has been finalized. Agreement with its wording is unanimous. Formal action yesterday by the legislatures of Utah and Oregon brought to fifty the number of states calling for an Article V Convention to consider and pass the amendment. The convention has been scheduled for April 15th in Philadelphia. Subsequent quick ratification by at least thirty-eight states is expected.

## The Last Amendment

*Section 1. The entirety of the Constitution of the United States of America, its articles and amendments collectively and all authority therein, shall expire on the fifth anniversary of the ratification of this amendment (Expiration). At Expiration, all assets, liabilities, rights, claims, obligations, equities, powers, privileges, and anything else belonging to or subject to the United States of America shall be assumed in full by the several states.*

*Section 2. Upon ratification of this amendment, the several states shall commission and vest their authority in a body (Agency) which shall manage all matters related to Expiration. The Agency shall have accountability only to the several states and shall be free from all jurisdictions and authorities (legislative, executive, and judicial) of the government of the United States of America. The Agency may designate deputies who shall be, with respect to this amendment, forever immune from prosecution for Treason, Sedition, Subversion, Conspiracy, Espionage, or any other crime against the United States of America.*

*Section 3. No later than two years from the ratification of this amendment, all the several states shall have aligned themselves by signed treaty or pact into two distinct confederations (Alignment). Else, this amendment is repealed. Subsequent to Alignment, a withdrawal, or attempted withdrawal, by any state from its chosen distinct confederation shall not be cause for the repeal of this amendment.*

*Section 4. No later than four years from the ratification of this amendment, each of the two distinct confederations of states shall have, by its own devices, established and ratified its own constitution ordaining a democratic form of government for its own self-rule. Else, this amendment is repealed.*

*Section 5. A national referendum shall be administered on the first Saturday in July during each full calendar year between the year of ratification of this amendment and the year of Expiration. At each referendum, voters shall be polled "Shall the amendment to expire the Constitution of the United States of America be repealed?" Should greater than fifty percent of votes cast in the first referendum, greater than fifty-five percent of votes cast in the second referendum, greater than sixty percent of votes cast in the third referendum, or greater than sixty-five percent of votes cast in the fourth referendum be in the affirmative, this amendment is repealed.*

I am no longer surprised, but still am amazed, by how far

we have come. Your wise counsel has been integral to the process. Thank you.

With warmest regards, yours faithfully,

Geoff

# 16

May 11, 2019

Happy 20<sup>th</sup> birthday, Bee. I hope your examinations have gone well enough to allow for some celebrating the end of your teen years. I'm so very proud of your academic achievements. You've never let anything slow you down. Don't be discouraged by the professor who marginalized you. She's one of those who are bothered when someone they think is broken doesn't act broken. It's because the strength you demonstrate and the unfading brightness of your spirit illuminate the many cracks in her foundation. Someday she'll realize how your courage blesses her.

Thank you for braving the rain to ride out to me last month. I apologize for not making clear while you were here how much I enjoyed your visit. It wasn't until after you'd left that I fully appreciated your parting directive to "keep living." You correctly sensed and boldly confronted my resignation. I admitted to myself that I have indeed let myself go these past several months. But I've now shaven my beard (besides its wild incivility I could tell it complicated your lip reading), cleaned this place up (perhaps not to Grandma's standards, but a drastic improvement nonetheless), and started eating better. I'm resolved to sustain these gains and you deserve the credit.

A few days ago I visited Grandma's grave. I knew you'd been there by the bundle of flowers. They were wilted but I could still see they were that kind you like so much. My time with Grandma was more special knowing you had preceded me. You are a bundle of flowers that never wilts. You are my Songbird.

With all my love,

Grandpa

# 17

June 10, 2019

Dear Bart:

Ratification is imminent, perhaps complete by the time you read this. The process has not been much of a debate, but more of a race to thirty eight. Conservatives are off and running with "Federation of American States." Liberals continue haggling over their name, though all the most likely options include "commonwealth."

Regarding capital cities, Washington D.C. seems likely to remain the liberals' Mecca. Conservatives, on the other hand, are rallying around Independence, Kansas. Underlying logic includes the town being nestled in the southeast corner of a red state in the middle of a sea of red states. Also, Independence is small and well off the beaten path, making it a municipality not readily capable of sustaining an extensive bureaucratic machine. And the choice exudes a powerful symbolic allure – a nation headquartered in an idyllic rural pastureland leaves little doubt of that society's underlying value set. The city's name is a cherry on top. Of course, either nation's official choice of capital city will have to wait until the Section 3 alignment is concluded. If the speed of ratification is any indicator, however, that could happen quite quickly.

I have been asked to consider an executive leadership post in the Section 2 Agency. Naturally, it would require my resignation from Congress. Back in February you cautioned me only to become involved if I felt there was "purpose and nobility" in this cause. I believe there is both. Beth believes likewise. In the same letter you also offered me your help. Bart, please retire from your retirement and come join me, wherever that may be and whatever that may look like. I am confident we could construct an arrangement that suits you completely. Trust that with great joy and sincerity I will correspond with you forever, regardless what you choose, but I so miss the warmth of your presence and the fire of your spirit. Deny me, deny the world, no longer. Come back to us.

Yours affectionately,

Geoff

# 18

June 15, 2019

Geoff:

Thanks for the update. I must confess I've ridden into town several times this past week to check on the amendment's status. Shopkeeper Jay shares little snippets here and there. He's careful not to say too much, I think fearful I'll storm out and never return (my modest but regular demand for canned goods, coffee, and pipe tobacco is meaningful for the poor fellow's operation). He's a simple man, uneducated and poverty-practical. And he's good, small-town good, upbringing-good, the kind of good that'd compel you to entrust your family to him. Most of the time he's just patter, but sometimes he'll strike chords of tremendous depth and wisdom. Yesterday, for instance, he was lamenting the fate of those whose identity, purpose, and power seems doomed with the expiration of the United States. He spoke of the moderate politicians, that is "stand-for-nothing" Democrats and Republicans who've long disgruntled their hard-core bases by devotion to unprincipled compromise and so who now seem destined to be treated as lepers in purely liberal and purely conservative governments, viewed as misfits in either of the two new ideologically-honed bureaucracies. He also spoke of the "leaches" – Washington lawyers, accountants, consultants, lobbyists, etc. – who have engorged themselves on the perpetually bleeding system. He sagely predicted that partisan gridlock (the anticoagulant) will be much harder to come by in the new paradigm.

No surprise the liberals favor staying home in Washington. Independence is sensible for the conservatives, though something along the Gulf or Florida coastlines seems wiser. Yes, everything hinges on alignment. I'm curious how the states will choose sides, whether blue/red Electoral College patterns manifest when the stakes are so permanent.

Also no surprise you're being courted to help lead the bisection agency. I'm flattered by the invitation to join you but remain fully committed to my hermitage. Peaceful seclusion, penetrated only and occasionally by letters to and from a beloved few, is "the arrangement which suits me completely." If you truly need a Scattercorn at your side, Bee might be persuaded to join you. She graduates next May, likely with honor in two degrees – math and economics. I can't (and shouldn't) speak for her but I promise she'd take my career guidance to heart. And, selfishly, I'd be comforted knowing she's safe within the realm of your noble providence. There's no greater compliment I can pay you, my friend.

Bart

# 19

June 16, 2019

After church the whole family went and spent the day at Killarney. The campground was full but we had the kitchen and main cabin to ourselves. It was a wonderful day – warm, sunny, and Grandpa came. Everyone was so glad to see him, and he seemed truly happy to be with us. He still is too thin but he had shaven and combed his hair and dressed nicely.

The amendment was officially ratified at noon and Father asked Grandpa to say some words by the flagpole after lunch. Grandpa pointed up and said that five years from today that flag will become meaningless but what it stands for will never be. He said we all are nation builders now and must take the responsibility seriously. Then he said how much today would have meant to Grandma, with everyone coming together as a family. He noted it has been over nine months since she died. He said he still misses her very much. He said he wonders every day why God would take her first and leave him behind. This made me so sad I had to look down at the ground so he would not see my face. When I looked back up he had stopped talking. I wish Grandpa did not feel that way. At least it was good having him act like the head of the family again.

In the afternoon the boys and our cousins played volleyball on the beach then rented canoes. Everyone wanted me or Victoria in their canoe because they knew no one would flip us. I went with Philip and Matthew. It was only minutes before the boys started splashing and trying to tip each other over. No one tipped our canoe over but I got drenched in all the splashing. Peter's boat got flipped many times. He kept standing up and using his paddle to push others away but this made his boat top-heavy. I saw Philip call him a fat ass and Peter became very angry. This just made him fall out of his boat again. Everyone in boats and on shore was laughing. It was difficult not to!

Later Father asked me to join him and Grandpa on a stroll to the dam. They talked with each other while I walked between them. I did not bother trying to watch their lips. It was enough just to be with them. Father acts much younger when he is with Grandpa. He acts less worried about things, less anxious about his responsibilities, like he knows he is safe with Grandpa and that everything will be fine. This is evidence of what a father means to a son.

Grandpa departed before dinner was ready. No one wanted him to go but no one tried to stop him. I made sure I said goodbye last because I did not want him to be embarrassed. I could tell he was only mouthing his words to me, that no sound was coming out. I am his songbird, he said. I told him God must have left him behind because there is still a purpose in his staying. Then I told him I loved him and kissed his cheek. His eyes were closed as he nodded then he turned away and left.

After dinner I sat with Mother down by the water. We watched the shadows of the trees stretch over the lake. It was wonderful to be alone with her. I miss her while I am at school. I can tell she is relieved by Matthew's graduation. She is justified feeling satisfaction in bringing all five of us to adulthood, especially in these times. I told her this and she laughed. I so enjoy the sincerity of Mother's laugh. It looks like warm water feels. She warned me that her sisters are asking if I have found anyone yet. If they only understood the weight and thickness of my veil they would not attempt applying their templates to my life.

# 20

June 30, 2019

Geoff:

I've spent the last week working on the barn. Getting it in order is the last thing I remember Ruth asking me to do before she died. I'm sure she'd have given me a reprieve to mourn her but September 1st will be a year and I'm just as sure she'd be giving me hell for waiting a full twelve months to tackle my chores. The days are long and warm and are making for solid progress. It's true that the body fuels the mind and it turns out an old body fuels an old mind just as well. Moving junk and shoveling mummified horse shit has yielded perspective on the Bisection Inc. employee attraction and retention challenges you've mentioned. You're undoubtedly developing approaches for each but in case anyone wonders what old Scratchy would say…

Compensation/salary structure needs to be very for-profit (goal attainment) oriented, like what the best-in-class Fortune 500 companies use, not at all the traditional public service (seniority) model. It'd be wise to liberally utilize performance bonuses for hitting targets, milestones, etc., with efficiency of process and quality of product in mind. I was glad to see you use "clients" as pseudonym for the

F.A.S. and G.A.C. because that's what they are for the next five years – your customers. Impressing them and advancing their strategies should be lucrative (perhaps even highly lucrative) for B.S.I. employees since their employer will dissolve by design at Expiration.

While compensation/salary structure should be decidedly private sector, fringe benefits should imitate the public sector, i.e. be generous and absolute. Again, the company will dissolve at Expiration so you'll only attract and retain top-notch individuals if you ensure that they and their loved ones are in every reasonable way secure during their fleeting tenure with you.

With regard to retirement, aggressively backloading seems prudent. Figure out the right platform (401k match, defined benefit pension, or combination of the two – taking full advantage of the fact you're not bound by any IRS rules or federal statutes) then make both the company match and vesting schedule advance on a non-linear scale from years 1 through 5. For example, working a full Year 3 would count as 5 years of employment, a full Year 4 would count as 10 years, and a full Year 5 would count as 15 years. Something like that. It'd also be wise, then, to secure both clients' agreement to have time served at B.S.I. count toward their own bureaucracies' benefits programs. That would help entice B.S.I. talent to roll into F.A.S. and G.A.C. governments post-Expiration.

They want you to head the Department of International Associations, huh? If you accept, I don't envy you because you'll certainly have your hands full dealing with tyrants, warlords, and dictators (plus, then, all the Third World's leaders) but I've always said you're a silver-tongued devil. International diplomacy suits you and you'll do just fine.

In your letters you seem energized and optimistic about the world again. If you are then I am.

Happily blistered and aching,

Bart

# 21

July 3, 2019

Bee:

Killarney was bittersweet, but you were right, far more sweet than bitter. I'm glad you talked me into going. I shudder to think what I'd become without your tender ministrations.

I've learned that Geoffrey Braddock, my old congressman friend and only other regular correspondent, is likely to become a high-level leader at the newly chartered Bisection Inc. It appears B.S.I. will be based in Washington D.C. Geoff is a man of tremendous character – bright, articulate, and honorable. He has two daughters (both a little older than you) over whom he fawns, and his wife Beth is an absolute dear. I respect your free will and appreciate you're now considering graduate school, but take this employment suggestion to heart: Geoff's mentorship, especially at a place and during a time of such historical significance, would be meaningful in the highest degree. It's also worth noting that Geoff will probably be joined at B.S.I. by several of his Congressional staff, including some young folks he speaks of very highly. Between now and your graduation next May, please simply consider the possibilities.

The other day while cleaning the barn I came across one of those little black velvet pouches in which you used to hide hand-written notes. Do you remember doing that? The pouch was tacked to a rafter way up in the loft. I laughed imagining little Bee crawling way up there with hammer and nail in hand. The cinch was loose and I could see the folded-up paper inside. Curiosity nearly got the best of me, but I left the pouch in place and the note untouched. The next time you visit, perhaps we can take down the pouch and read the note together? I can't help wondering about the secrets within…

Love you,

Grandpa

# 22

July 9, 2019

Dear Bart:

I appreciate your input with respect to Bisection Inc. compensation and benefits. We were in fact already carefully considering each point mentioned, but your rationale (and implied endorsement) is certainly useful in our continuing discernments. Thank you.

In the two weeks since B.S.I.'s chartering we have made great progress finding a home for and shaping the organization. I am amazed by the fifty states' collective efficiency and can-do spirit in this regard. Ironically, it is the act of complete and permanent divorce which finally brings conservatives and liberals together in harmonious, cheerful production. The wisdom of your farewell charge seems validated. Here is where we stand at present:

We have arranged to purchase approximately two hundred acres of the National Arboretum from the U.S. Department of Agriculture. Several access roads wind their way through the trees and converge at the property's high point. There sit two structures – a 1940's observatory and a 1970's bioscience lab. The observatory is dilapidated and useless but the lab building is large and will be renovated.

Two brand new office buildings are to be built in close proximity to the lab. All construction will commence immediately. Some in Congress are balking at the notion of B.S.I. sitting less than three miles from the Capitol, but after ratification their resistance is futile.

It looks as if B.S.I. will consist of nine departments – Coexistence, Economic Systems, Infrastructure, Intangible Assets, International Associations, Laws & Justice, Military Assets, Natural Resources, and Tangible Assets. The general purpose of each is to be as follows:

Coexistence – to manage the Section 3 Alignment process, coordinate the drafting and ratification (Section 4) of constitutions for the Federation of American States and the Great American Commonwealth, administer the Section 5 referenda, facilitate border agreements and policies, and address anything and everything else that might affect post-Expiration harmony between the F.A.S. and the G.A.C.

Economic Systems – to split the national debt, model-out various monetary policies and strategies for printing currency, facilitate debate for methods of pegging currencies, retool and reengineer the stock exchanges, set banking rules, and so on. Economic Systems will also handle anything having to do with fair business practices and antitrust, anything over which the F.T.C. or S.E.C. currently have jurisdiction, e.g. domain of the Sherman and Clayton Acts. They also will screen existing statutes and executive orders for relevance with respect to the clients' eventual constitutions and make recommendations as to how (and/or if) the clients should legislate the matter.

Infrastructure – to manage the handoff of all D.O.T. contracts and jurisdictions, i.e. bridges, roads, airports, railways, waterways. Also to coordinate bisection of utility systems (gas lines, power plants, electric grid) and other Department of Energy matters, plus telephone/cell networks, cable, and fiber optic hardware.

Intangible Assets – to determine how best to sort out and disseminate rights from patents, trademarks, trade secrets, and copyrights, i.e. all matters of intellectual property. Everyone agrees that pre-Expiration I.P. rights need to be respected and both clients will want their I.P. systems smartly designed and in sync with each other.

International Associations – to address treaties, tariffs, matters of extradition and rendition, global affiliations, and all other matters currently within the realm of the State Department. I have been formally offered and officially accepted the role as head ("vice president") of this department. My resignation from Congress is imminent.

Laws and Justice – to facilitate the design and construction of legal systems for the F.A.S. and G.A.C. I expect this will be a very difficult-to-manage department because the clients have such different philosophies with respect to the role of the judiciary. The two constitutions will spell out the exact frameworks, of course, but Laws and Justice personnel will have to fill in the gaps. They will also be tasked with bisecting the federal prison system and marshalling its tenants. Professional certifications for doctors, lawyers, and accountants will need to be addressed, as will any corporations, companies, or partnerships that wish to change their state of incorporation so as to be headquartered in the other country.

Military Assets – to bisect the United States' military, its hardware, its software, its bases around the world, its Intelligence services (C.I.A., N.S.A. etc.), its space command, satellite fleet, N.A.S.A., and so on, all while carefully coordinating with the president who, until the exact moment of Expiration, remains responsible for preserving, protecting, and defending the Constitution (and thereby the people) of the United States of America. Staffing this department rightfully requires great care and contemplation.

Natural Resources – to develop transition plans for things such as drilling rights and logging permits, as well as standards for air and water quality which are amenable to each client. Also to bear responsibility for determining uptake rights for common watersheds, rivers, lakes, and reservoirs. As a general rule, Natural Resources will manage anything and everything germane to the U.S. Department of Agriculture (land-use plans, subsidized loans, etc.) and the U.S. Environmental Protection Agency.

Tangible Assets – to divide up all physical assets of the United States government – buildings and their contents, museum artifacts, any and all non-military vehicles, cars, trucks, airplanes, Treasury's printing presses, gold bullion, Post Offices, IRS computers, etc. Tangible Assets appraisers will assign value to everything so that its accountants can help the clients distribute it all equitably.

Bart, regarding your granddaughter, I would be honored to speak with her at any time about a role at Bisection Inc. These are unprecedented times and this is an unprecedented organization so I cannot make any guarantees as to its ultimate work culture. But I can guarantee you, and I will, that Bee would be in good hands if she were to earn and accept a position on my team. I have invited a select few from my congressional staff to join me at B.S.I. Each can be a meaningful friend for Bee, I think Joe especially.

Like anyone, Bee would have to win the role based on merit, character, and integrity. Though knowing the stock from which she comes, her odds are as short as can be. A friend of yours is a friend of mine. A beloved of yours is a beloved of mine. Please share Bee's wishes and I will offer every possible consideration.

Always yours respectfully,

Geoff

# 23

September 1, 2019

Dear Bart:

The Department of Coexistence has completed plans for Realignment and the states have approved. It may be a few more weeks before news is made public so I thought you would appreciate a sneak peek.

The process will be straightforward for the thirty-five states which have been fairly consistently either blue or red in presidential elections over the past sixty years. Each of these states will administer a simple "F.A.S. or G.A.C.?" referendum. A return of at least fifty-five percent shall be considered definitive. Should neither side achieve the fifty-five percent threshold in the first go-round, a second referendum would be held three months later, then with a simple majority being definitive. However, in each of these thirty-five states, polling for the dominant ideology is currently at or above sixty percent so very few second referenda are expected.

Sorting the fifteen purple states will be more complicated, as they have been vacillating between blue and red for decades and the amendment now requires each to permanently commit one way or the other. Compelling millions of people to acquiesce to the political ideology of millions of people "plus one" is likely to prove problematic. The solution is to have each purple state administer up to eight referenda, separating each by just one month. Ballots in any one of the first seven referenda will list three choices: "F.A.S.," "G.A.C.," and "Undecided." Ballots in an eighth and final referendum will list only two choices: "F.A.S." and "G.A.C." If either "F.A.S." or "G.A.C." secures at least fifty-five percent of the votes in three consecutive of the first seven referenda, it becomes a state's Alignment choice. However, if neither "F.A.S." nor "G.A.C." secures at least fifty-five percent of the votes in three consecutive of the first seven referenda, then a simple majority in the eighth referendum shall be definitive.

The purple state process funnels citizens quickly toward a mutually exclusive choice between ideological destinations. The psychology is deliberate – every voter knows a single winner must inevitably be chosen from a shrinking list of candidates. And, as it is with papal elections, voters will be cognoscente of "who's winning" and "by how much" as the process unfolds. We believe these realities make support for an implausible candidate (i.e. "Undecided") ever more foolhardy. There is no consensus expectation for how or how quickly the purple states will choose. My personal guess is that most will align by their fourth or fifth referendum, and that a "sudden death" eighth will prove to be the exception.

National bisection seems more certain than ever, perhaps fated. The great precipice grows closer.

Wishing you well, I am yours most fondly,

Geoff

# 24

·

May 11, 2020

Today the church of trees, off Chisholm Road. It was a most memorable birthday. I will never forget. I approached on the trail Father used when we were little. The way was not difficult. At the top of the little hill I looked down and saw that no one was there. I was glad to be alone.

I went and sat down on one of the pews. They are still made from long tree trunks cut in half lengthwise. I noticed the pew ahead of me was perfectly balanced atop its center log. The left and right support logs were missing. I did not see them anywhere. Yet the pew was stable atop just the center one. No other pews were missing support logs.

I looked skyward. The canopy was full and lush green in the sunlight. A strong wind was pushing the branches so that they danced. This was entrancing and I spent several minutes enjoying the sight of the dancing branches. Then I found it odd because there had been no wind while I walked through the woods. Why would the wind suddenly be with me in the church? The wind. Why does it haunt me so? I appreciated that the dancing branches and wind must be making a glorious sound together. For the first time in a long long time I let myself be sad for not hearing. I grew weak and let it in. I closed my eyes as the sadness flooded me. The sadness reigned, and my pride was defeated. In that impenetrable silent darkness which is mine alone, I surrendered. I asked with all my heart to be complete just for an instant, to be able to hear the wind and the branches for just one second, one second being long enough to remember the sound for a lifetime. And then into my silent darkness came not the rush of wind or the whoosh of leaves but a man's voice. With my ears I heard this man's voice say "twenty seven." With my ears I heard this! I opened my eyes and jumped up and looked all around. I saw no one anywhere but the sound of that man's voice lingered, hovered, sharp and fresh. I know it had been my ears that heard it. I know it. They had opened momentarily. Again there was the silence but my mind held the sound alive, it holds it still, now and for all time. "Twenty seven" he had said slowly and reflectively.

Curious, but filled with hope, I looked toward the fieldstone altar. The old cross is the same as when I was a little girl, just as grayed and pitted and gnarled. I stared at it for a very long time with the sound of "twenty seven" playing over and over in my mind. Then through the cross, past it, I saw the glittering of metal. Hanging from a low branch in a tree beyond were wind chimes. I went and studied them closely. There were seven brass tubes on the bottom. Above them spun a thin disk of glinting silver. It was the size of a salad plate and revolved slowly to the wind-driven gyrations of the tubes below. On the disk was carved the figure of an angel. Her exquisite wings fanned out to each side. Her hands were pressed together in prayer and held up against her face. Her eyes were closed and peaceful. She was very beautiful.

As I stood watching the chimes, I realized the tubes must be making a wonderful sound. I longed to hear them too, but my prayer had already been answered and I am sustained. The sound in my ears of the man saying "twenty seven" was a miracle. It must have been the angel who delivered it.

# 25

July 4, 2020

Today is the first referendum. All the Unitists need is fifty percent and the amendment will be repealed, but no one believes they have a chance. There is no middle anymore. There is only left and right, and they are together in this. The advertisements are endless. Some are very well done. They depict American history and our accomplishments. But I do not believe many minds will change. I went and asked Grandpa how he will vote and he said however I tell him. He smiled to hide his sadness. Or maybe it was not sadness, but regret, regret at being the spark to all of this. If there is regret, there must be anger too. It is odd. He is so simple in form and ways, yet still a deep and most complicated man.

I received a message saying I have been assigned to Dr. Michelle Hamilton for my masters program. Her record in econometrics is impressive. She is broadly published and appears to consult often for the private sector. I will go meet her in person as soon as possible, but without letting her know I am coming. I will introduce myself while watching her eyes closely. They never lie.

This afternoon I went back to the church of trees. The beautiful praying angel was gone and I did not hear the man's voice. I was disappointed but am no less certain of the miracle. I have told no one about it, not even Grandpa. This is my own mystery. There are so very many questions.

# 26

December 7, 2020

Dear Bart:

I apologize for the long pause in writing. Expiration's lopsided win in July yielded quite a stimulating effect on Bisection Inc. That first referendum seemed the one most likely to unravel our endeavors, and a simple majority of the popular vote would have done it. But nearly seventy-five percent declined repeal and the bar for Unitists gets steadily higher from here. This reality has greatly intensified our engagement with every facet of B.S.I.'s purpose. Furthermore, the completion of construction on two new buildings, impressive renovation of a third, and hustled relocation of all nine B.S.I. departments into the National Arboretum complex has been quite a distraction. Though my excuses are numerous, and legitimate every one, my delinquency in writing you is most unacceptable for so trusted a friend. I am sorry.

My penance is two-fold. First, I offer you a final accounting of Alignment. Early this morning Section 3 of the amendment was fulfilled when Florida concluded its seventh referendum, selecting the Federation of American States for the third time in as many months. Therefore the F.A.S. will include all of Dixie – Virginia, West Virginia,

Kentucky, Tennessee, North and South Carolina, Georgia, Florida, Alabama, Mississippi, Louisiana, and Arkansas. Joining them will be Midwesterners in Iowa, Missouri, and Indiana, plus citizens of the sun-baked expanses of the Southwest – Texas, Oklahoma, New Mexico, Arizona, and Nevada. The Mountain West states – Utah, Colorado, Wyoming, Idaho, and Montana – will join the breadbaskets of Kansas and Nebraska, plus both Dakotas. Alaska rounds out the F.A.S. stable.

The twenty states of the Great American Commonwealth will straddle the continent. Maine, New Hampshire, Vermont, Connecticut, Massachusetts, Rhode Island, New York, Delaware, New Jersey, and Maryland will form its footprint in the Northeast. Ohio will bridge Pennsylvania to Michigan, while Illinois, Wisconsin, and Minnesota will anchor the G.A.C. in the Upper Midwest. The G.A.C. will boast the entire Pacific coastline – Washington, Oregon, and California – as well as Hawaii.

Contemplating this map raises plenty of questions, the foremost of which are all challenges of discontinuousness. The Department of Coexistence has been hard at work attempting to mitigate, if not prevent entirely, the most obvious border and logistical complications. More importantly, now that the states have formally aligned, drafting of constitutions (Section 4) will begin in earnest. In that regard I will of course keep you informed as best I can.

My second offering of contrition is a solicitation for perspective on a rather critical diplomatic matter. As we continue passing mileposts on the road to Expiration, the world community is growing ever more anxious about how to handle international agreements to which the United States is a party. This is a truly unprecedented problem – the signatory to a treaty or accord disappearing, essentially ceasing to exist, vanishing from the earth, and then being replaced by two completely new offspring nations. What exactly are the obligations, if any, of the offspring nations with respect to treaties entered into by their parent? It is being widely debated, and with great passion, but ultimately there can be only one conclusion: neither the F.A.S. nor the G.A.C. can be force-bound to a treaty their yet-to-be-formed governments have not considered. Dissenters are short on logic and devoid of recourse. I have no doubt they will (must) acquiesce to reason in due course.

However, the global community of nations cannot ignore the collective economic, social, and military might of what will likely soon become the F.A.S. and G.A.C. While it will ultimately be agreed that the two new nations cannot be pre-bound to agreements made by their parent, it is already agreed that they should not be encouraged to walk away, either. I have therefore proposed, and am in the process of defending, a concept to address this. I call it Reestablishment. Essentially, any and all international agreements to which the United States has been a party, whether bilateral or multilateral in nature, would be reopened to all signatories for reconsideration. In every case the F.A.S. and G.A.C. would be invited to the table as separate, sovereign co-heirs of the United States of America and expected to consider the agreement via whatever ways and means their respective constitutions eventually spell out. In parallel, all the original signatories of the agreement would consider it anew.

Obviously the pitfalls are plentiful – the temptations to alter and amend original wording will be great. But, if administered correctly, Reestablishment should exact a "peer pressure" (explicit, implicit, rightful, and extreme) on nations not to unwind or otherwise disintegrate the longstanding tenet agreements which have embedded relative peace and general prosperity throughout the modern era. Reestablishment should, figuratively speaking, allow us to remove a brick from a wall and replace it with two smaller bricks, all with minimal risk of cracking or collapsing the wall. As to this, and in every other regard, I am most glad for your wisdom.

With warmest wishes, yours affectionately,

Geoff

# 27

May 17, 2021

Dear Grandpa:

I was so glad to see you on my birthday. No gift was sweeter than that. Father believes you are healthy and happy. Mother disagrees. She believes you are healthy but sad. I believe you are healthy and happy to be sad. You punish yourself, Grandpa. There is no reason for it. You once told me sadness is selfish. Be generous again.

My marks were perfect this year. Dr. Hamilton says my thesis is progressing well and that I am on track to receive my master's degree next May. She has been most supportive. She said she is glad to move me into a PhD program if I wish. I wonder, though, if it is time for me to journey into the world, out from under the trees and into the open spaces. I do not know what to do, honestly. School suits me, the mathematics specifically. Perhaps that is why I linger on, because I am so fond of numbers. They are forthright and honest, indiscriminate and unwavering. And they are silent. Numbers are soundless. Numbers make no noise whatsoever. Their cousins, the notes, do. But numbers do not need to be heard to be understood or appreciated. The absoluteness of their meaning is discernible without a sound, as it is with anything I love.

As it is with you, Grandpa.

Now you know of my miracle. I was grateful for the calm you exhibited as I told you. Please help me understand. I must know why one number broke the rules, why one number rang out in my ears and stained my mind. At first it was his voice that mattered, the deliverer's, the impossibility of its registry. But now it is the parcel itself, stark before me and unfading. The complete lack of either clue or context is as frustrating as the riddle itself, as is its lone revelation. I have failed to determine an earthly remedy, and so I wonder. Could the funny little man assist me?

Bee

# 28

July 3, 2021

I am writing from beneath a sweetgum tree beside a fast-moving creek at the base of King's Mountain. It is a sunny morning and already quite warm. It should be very hot by the time I reach the summit this afternoon, and I am glad. Today is the second referendum. Now the threshold for repeal is fifty-five percent. The amendment will never be overturned. Most are already planning for life after Expiration. They are intoxicated by the promise of like-minded utopia, but I do not think it is good. Uniformity of thought eventually requires oppression.

Resting at an overlook about two-thirds up the mountain. The heat of the day is indeed making it difficult. Mother would enjoy me confessing my legs hurt. She was right in saying college softened me up. But she would also say I am an Appalachian girl and I was born to climb. There are a few people here and there, more headed down than up.

It is about noon and I am at the summit. I have found what must be Grandpa's outcropping, what he called the nifty spot. It is not obvious. It is mostly screened from view by a cluster of pines but it must be the place. I will eat my lunch here then walk out onto it and wait for the funny little man. There is no wind. I am surprised to be this high and feel no breeze at all. The sun is baking the rock. It is extremely hot, and I am glad.

It is 5 p.m. and he has not come. I am sunburned and chilled, I think from dehydration. When the spells of lightheadedness and fatigue come, I close my eyes to see if that will bring him. I will continue waiting.

I just woke. It is 7:40 p.m. I did not mean to sleep so long but my head was hurting badly. I drank my water and am feeling better. This outcropping is now in the long shadows. There is a little while left before sunset. I am sure he would have waited for me if I had been sleeping.

A beautiful bird has landed on the rock near me, arm's reach away. I do not recognize the variety. It is late in the evening for a bird to be out unsheltered. The movement of my writing does not scare it away. Its beak is open. It is singing to me. It does not know its song is wasted. Why has the funny little man not come? So many care about so little, and a great many care about nothing at all. Why would he not oblige just one who cares so much?

In the remaining light I can see a ranger making his way up the trail. If he discovers me I know he will direct me down the mountain. But I will hide and wait for full dark and make my way down alone. A descent through the trees at night does not frighten me. My only fear is reaching the end without learning the answer.

# 29

November 4, 2021

Geoff, my dear friend, how are you? You're often quoted these days and I enjoy it. I proudly reminded shopkeeper Jay you were my protégé back in Congress, that it was I who taught you how to be that smooth and charming. He just shook his head and laughed, the wise old shit. There's plenty of dust on me now, plenty of cobwebs. I scared myself yesterday. First I got lost briefly out in the flats, the rocky land in the far west of my property. I knew where I was generally, but I couldn't remember which direction led home. Studying shadows for a while got me oriented. Still it rattled me because for seven decades I've known that piece of earth like the back of my hand. Then on the trail home I walked past the clearing where Ruth and I used to watch deer. I couldn't remember her maiden name, not for the life of me. It's been over three years. I sat down against a tree and cried like a baby. It wasn't me losing my mind that saddened me, it was forgetting a piece of her like that. God I love her. Long spans go by during which I don't think about her. Then it hits me hard, like a tidal wave. I knew my retirement was the second to last stake in the ground. I'm somewhere along the short line to the end. I'm conscious of my heart beating now. I feel it in there thumping away. I wonder how many ticks are left. When will it have had enough? Such a thankless job. It's gone on so tirelessly for so long, the stubborn old thing. I stopped crying when I remembered. Steiner.

I didn't write you just to prove my insanity. I also wanted to share some perspective on the F.A.S. draft constitution. Neither the brevity of the document nor the speed of its development surprises me. A conservative bible should, after all, articulate only the very few things its government may do to its people, implicitly delegating the great balance of authorities, powers, and responsibilities to individual citizens. However, I see some serious pitfalls with the work as it's currently worded. No one's likely to give a damn anymore what I think. Nevertheless…

Several structural elements apparently designed to ensure the government's efficiency and strict compliance with the will of the people could actually create societal instability. A unicameral federal legislature filled with term-limited representatives means amateurs will be doing the lawmaking. Three years is better than two as a term of office, but what other industry in the world force-retires its most successful after just twelve years? How effective can a nation's sole deliberative body be when its most senior, most experienced leaders are banished so quickly? Add to that the constitutionally-mandated sunsetting of every law at ten years and the article enabling a popular vote overturn of any law or regulation and you have the makings of chaos. Industries plan capital investments on twenty and thirty year cycles. Institutions invest with generational transitions in mind. How can the many facets of a nation operate strategically if its legal underpinnings and regulatory matrices are set in sand? I appreciate the need to prevent political tyranny and to neuter overzealous bureaucracy, but legislating with novices, making their laws transient, and giving the general public on-second-thought veto power seems just as perilous.

I must admit, I smiled rather broadly upon reading the clause making F.A.S. judges impeachable by direct popular vote. The United States judiciary's routine casting away of fashionable legislation and executive orders has equally riled both left and right over two centuries of American history. However, I believe a democracy needs its judges to be practically untouchable, free from any political consequences of their decisions, so as to prevent might from making right. If the (all too often) undiscerning masses have easy means of removing judges who deviate from popular sentiment, then it shall be the mob – not the law – which rules.

The ten percent cap ("civic tithe") on any citizen's total tax burden seems difficult enough for the F.A.S. to sustain fiscally, let alone police administratively. It would be far wiser to codify this guarantee in statutory form, rather than enshrining it as constitutional right, since in times of national crisis the collective cost and goodwill necessary for expediently amending the Constitution might not be readily spared.

Nothing troubles me more than the article on voter eligibility. Its phraseology seems to grant voting rights only to those citizens who've paid more in aggregate into the F.A.S. coffers than they've taken in aggregate out of them. "Net takers" would apparently be denied the right to vote so long as they're in the red, presumably because it's unfair or immoral to allow freeloaders to vote themselves into their neighbor's pocketbook. I'll say it plainly – there will be no effective defense of or advocacy for the poor and underprivileged if they have zero electoral currency. This concept is inhumane, uncompassionate, disgraceful, and brazenly un-American. I hope to God it is removed.

On a personal note, Bee says she's done with school in May. She'll have her master's in econometrics. If you have a vacancy on your staff, please consider her. I promise you won't be sorry.

Yours,

Bart

# 30

March 14, 2022

This morning I interviewed with Dr. Geoffrey Braddock for a fulltime position on his staff, commencing this summer. Dr. Braddock is currently head of the Department of International Associations at Bisection Incorporated. The role is to be based in Washington D.C. on the B.S.I. campus. Grandpa has always spoken most highly of Dr. Braddock so I was very glad to meet him in person.

As I approached his office he was standing ready in the threshold wearing a contented, welcoming expression. His suit coat was buttoned, his tie tight and straight, and his hands at his side. He is a powerful man, and a supremely busy one at that, yet there he stood, having set aside all those responsibilities for this relatively trivial task. Beyond inherent character, it was out of respect for Grandpa. Dr. Braddock honors his friends. He is loyal.

My host introduced us and Dr. Braddock smiled very warmly at me. Relaxation in his temples and brow perfectly complemented the comfortable exertion of his lips and jaw. Forced smiles are bottom-heavy, but his was authentic, balanced between soft eyes and happy mouth.

We shook hands. His was warm and soft. He gripped mine with respectful firmness, yet I could feel him subtly adjusting the pressure, seeking the right combination of professionalism and affection. To him, my comfort and self-confidence outweighed the need to establish alpha dominance. He is an excellent, considerate boss.

I kept my eyes on him while the host recounted the morning's events. It must have been a cordial, light-hearted synopsis because several times Dr. Braddock turned toward me with a look of polite amusement. He was clean shaven and his full head of graying hair was neatly combed. His teeth are slightly crooked and nowhere close to white. He is dignified but not vain. His complexion is fair and the skin on his face lined, bearing crow's feet and marks of long sun exposure. He grew up outdoors. His face is handsome and tender. It irradiates an extraordinary innate kindness. It is easy to stare at him. He is slightly shorter than average, solid in frame but fit.

He spoke to me, saying "It is a great pleasure to meet you, Bee. I hope you have been treated well?" Before answering I studied his eyes, watching for insincerity's high-speed fluttering. But his bluish gray irises were steady. Both the statement and question had been truthful.

As I followed him into his office I noted his aftershave, the old and spicy variety. It had been applied modestly, for its immediate curative effect, not as an attractant. He is both happily married and a creature of habit, finding comfort in routine.

He swiveled a smart-looking leather chair in my direction and politely invited me to sit by outstretching his hand. I quickly admired the quality of his suit. It had been tailor-made and was well-pressed. A whiff of starch meant a recent dry-cleaning for the dress shirt. His tie was silk, with beautiful pastels complementing the suit's faint pin striping. The silver tie tack matched his belt buckle which matched his watch. His wife selects his clothing.

He moved around to his side of the desk as I took my seat. I surveyed the décor. His office is warmly appointed and very personalized. He is renowned and accomplished yet the walls are devoid of ego trophies. Absent are shots of him posing with heads of state and kibitzing with world power brokers. Instead, there hang impromptu photographs of friends and family. There are silly drawings that make no sense, botched childhood art projects, conquered school exams (both A's and E's), a broken golf club, bronzed baby shoes, and a frayed old beach towel. These are the things that fill him up. These are things over which he can reminisce and tell stories and teach lessons. It is organic, perishable things that he loves. He knows he is mortal. Then I noticed the books, hundreds of them, mostly old. I breathed in their divine musty scent. One entire wall of his office is lined from floor to ceiling. He too is a bibliophile, appreciating the fermentation of thought into word.

He spent twenty minutes or so asking about my interests and hobbies. The rudimentary questions required minimal concentration, affording me ample opportunity to study his lips. His cadence is relaxed, the inflection Southern. He finishes words ending in "t" by snapping the tip of his tongue off his upper pallet. He enunciates words cleanly, like the well-educated man that he is. I wonder about the depth of his voice.

Then he switched gears, asking for permission to query me on my master's thesis. I said of course and asked if I may consult my notes. He happily agreed. I leaned forward to open my handbag and he immediately turned his head away, glancing casually out the window instead. He is a gentleman and the father of daughters.

We spent the balance of time discussing the nature of the job itself, its challenges, and the workplace dynamics at Bisection Inc. I believe he was impressed by my questions and answers. I asked him about a mentor or someone to help me get acclimated in the early going. He seemed energized by this and said he was glad I asked. He said he would place me under the watchful eye of his most faithful deputy, a young man named Joe. Dr. Braddock's face glowed after saying this. His breathing slowed and deepened. His posture straightened. He said "I would trust Joe with my life." Then he smiled very sincerely, mostly to himself. He loves the young man as a son.

I hope they offer me the position. In every way imaginable this seems the right next step in my journey.

# 31

May 11, 2022

Happy 23rd birthday, Bee. This old heart is beating happily knowing you'll be working for Geoff Braddock. Congratulations on winning the job, and on earning your master's degree. I couldn't be prouder of you. Geoff wrote me and shared how impressed he was with you during the interview. He said you exhibited poise and maturity far beyond your years, but that's no surprise to me. You can learn a great deal from him. Many are blessed with intelligence. Some mix it into knowledge. Few bake it into wisdom. He is one who does. Be assertive spending time in Geoff's presence. Carefully watch his ways and study his methods. Observe how respectfully he treats people, regardless of rank, worth, or credentials. He is a gifted leader whom people naturally love. You'll quickly sense, if you haven't already, why I'm so glad you're on his team.

Geoff's naturally modest and so won't share much about himself unless you ask, but you should. His family's hallmarks are many the same as ours. He grew up on a farm in a valley of the Blue Ridge, the southernmost swath of these same Appalachians. He once told me he was the only college graduate among his siblings (here again I roll my eyes at three of your brothers' half-assed efforts in higher education). I believe his undergraduate degree is political science. His doctorate is in history. He and his wife Beth met in graduate school. You'll love Beth. She is a marvelous woman – sweet, smart as a whip, and funny as hell. Anyway, Geoff's professorship at Washington & Lee lasted until he succumbed to fate and agreed to run for Congress. His thoughtful, unforced eloquence appealed well to the district's church barbeque personality and he handily throttled the grizzled, boorish incumbent. Geoff was in his earlier forties when he first arrived in Washington, but he seemed much younger. I was immediately drawn to his genuine vitality. He was a breath of fresh air in that place. Obviously he's been successful in politics but I know he's never stopped missing his role as a professor. He'll find joy in teaching you, Bee. Let him.

No man is perfect. Geoff's greatest fault is his tendency to be too soft, to over-trust the misbehaved, be too easy on the failing, and be too kind to the wicked. God may find this virtuous. I find it frustrating. Geoff knows I do and would probably laugh heartily at hearing you repeat it. Also, every man has a temper, and though I've never seen Geoff's in full bloom, I've witnessed him lose his cool on several occasions. He'll certainly bare his fangs in the presence of a bully. Perhaps he was pushed around as a boy, I don't know, but displays of illegitimate or overbearing power always sour his disposition. And he does have pets. I'm sure he doesn't do it consciously, and it doesn't seem to be toxic to the teams he leads, but he can't hide extra fondness or affection for a certain few.

This can limit his vision at times. Your powers of observation are acute. You'll be able to find Geoff's favorites in short order. You may very well end up being one yourself. If so, don't fret. There's no danger in it.

This will be your first real foray into the working world, Bee, and I have no doubt you'll execute your job responsibilities brilliantly. But don't go to Washington just to work. Go there to live as well. I know it angers you when your loved ones push and pressure you to get out more and date more and have more fun and so on. I appreciate, perhaps more than anyone, the extraordinary nature of your challenge and how it has shaped you. I understand, certainly more than anyone, you are haunted in ways the rest of us will never comprehend. You have chosen thus far to dwell in realms of mystic loneliness. With all my heart I hope you will choose differently from now on. With all my heart I hope that in the days I have left I will see you live and love fully. Open your heart to the beauty and joys of the regular world, Bee. Its flaws and ugliness drove me into seclusion, where I reside still. Don't be a coward like me. Live fully. Love fully.

Grandpa

# 32

June 2, 2022

Dear Bart:

Bee is confirmed to start with us on the thirteenth. Her cubical is ready, her training schedule mapped out, and her first few months' goals determined. As is our custom, I will introduce her to the entire department during mid-morning break that Monday. We very much look forward to her arrival. I assure you she will be warmly welcomed.

My other reason for writing is to share that I have been asked to address the press from the still-under-construction F.A.S. Capitol in Independence, Kansas on July 1st. The structure is impressive to behold – simultaneously grand and austere. The building stands at the end of a perfectly straight mile-long boulevard surrounded by flat, closely mown lawn, speckled here and there with trees. Wide sidewalks wind their way lazily alongside fountain-laden ponds and across robust block bridges spanning gurgling brooks. The grounds are park-like and beautiful. The Capitol's exterior is a collage of bricks in earthy-tones. Windows are plentiful and all of identical size. Each is recessed into the bricks handsomely and mirrored with a slightly golden hue. The building varies in height between two, three, and four stories but lacks any towers, domes, or spires. The structure conveys strength and permanence while also modest practicality. On the inside, large atria, marbled floors, and multistory hallways create a train-station feel. Most of the ceiling is glass, allowing sunlight to cascade throughout common chambers. Though ready for décor, most interior spaces remain barren pending the precise administrative needs of the F.A.S. government. A notable exception is the communications wing, including the main briefing room from which I will present.

The stated purpose of my address is to summarize the amendment's overall progress, then field questions on behalf of B.S.I. My leadership believes it wise to showcase developments in Independence, especially in light of the next day's vote. The third referendum's 60% threshold makes repeal a practical impossibility, but we do not wish to take anything to chance. Expiration's perceived inevitability might very well suppress pro-amendment turnout, regardless what current polling indicates, thereby tilting the playing field in favor of the Unitists. Beyond all else, therefore, I am to convey the worthiness, if not outright duty, of continuing to support Expiration by once again voting for it. I am working closely with Joe on the speech itself, but could use your help readying for the Q&A. There are a handful of prickly topics sure to be raised. Poring over "ideal" responses to each seems wise preparation. Drafted ideal responses follow. Please review and respond with perspective and suggestions. Confident you will reply, I expect your ruthless, unabashed feedback.

Regarding international criticism of either constitution:

For each nation, creating and refining its constitution has been expectantly, deliberately tedious. The ideological principles, civic structures, and governmental mechanisms reflected in each document have been very thoroughly, very conspicuously vetted for over three years. All the while Americans have been able to view current manifestations of each document online, watch editing in real-time, and in many cases even affect selection of phraseology via responses to flash-polling. Both processes have been transparently malleable in every respect. The F.A.S. Constitution – officially ratified this past March – and the G.A.C. Constitution – on pace to be ratified early next year – are inarguably the direct, undiluted reflections of the will of the people in each embryonic nation. Those in the international community may balk at certain aspects of each document if they wish, but neither the authenticity nor the democratic nature of these processes can be reasonably questioned.

Regarding Reestablishment:

It is appropriate for Bisection Inc., specifically its Department of International Associations, to lead Reestablishment activities since B.S.I. is the legal proxy for F.A.S. and G.A.C. interests on the global stage. As we contemplate Reestablishment, we are well aware the doctrine is meant to preserve the sanctity of hundreds of multinational agreements, some nearly five centuries old. Each agreement enables economic prosperity, domestic tranquility, military rules of engagement, border security, environmental stewardship, and so on. In aggregate, these treaties and accords serve as underpinnings of world peace. Therefore, a withdrawal from any would rightly indicate, both explicitly and symbolically, a rejection of the principles of peaceful coexistence between nations. A withdrawal could rightly be considered a knowing breach of trust between nations and deliberate provocation of destabilization.

Regarding the margins of support for Expiration in repeal referenda:

The amendment was affirmed by a popular vote of seventy-five percent in the first referendum and seventy-three percent in the second. In advance of tomorrow's third referendum, polls are indicating popular support for Expiration hovering between sixty-eight and seventy percent. If sixty-eight percent decline repeal, popular support for the amendment will have decayed a total of seven percentage points over a four year span. This is decay of only seven percentage points over four years, four years of fear mongering and apocalyptic predictions from the minority opposing Expiration. Furthermore, as expected, voter turnout has waned slightly over these four years. Supporters of Expiration have accepted its reality. Their urgency to go and vote for it has ebbed as they have moved on and begun planning for the new order. We have seen this acknowledged in referenda exit polling. However, those opposing the amendment have only strengthened in their resolve to see it undone. The relative passion of those working to defend versus working to defeat the amendment is stark, yet seven in ten Americans maintain their belief that Expiration must and will come to pass.

Regarding Expiration and threats against B.S.I., F.A.S., and G.A.C. leaders:

We are confident in the safety protocols and security procedures in place to defend B.S.I., F.A.S., and G.A.S. leaders. With respect to Expiration in the event of an attack on its personnel or institutions, let us appreciate anew that the Constitution is greater than any one individual, or any group of individuals. The Constitution has no corporeal form to harm or harass. The Constitution – the entire collection of parts, including Expiration – is a concept transcending the physical plane. The Constitution is affected, can only be affected, by the collective will of American citizens. The metamorphosis underway in this country is not a revolution. It is not a coup d'état. Revolutions and coups require particular human catalysts. Should those particular human catalysts be silenced, the revolutions and coups they lead are so silenced. Expiration has no human catalysts. Expiration is nothing more or less than an expression of the collective will of American citizens. Expiration is nothing more or less than democracy in action.

Bart, I am grateful for your wisdom.

Affectionately,

Geoff

# 33

June 13, 2022

My first day at Bisection Inc. I will never forget it. A woman named Marilyn greeted me as I entered. She explained she is Dr. Braddock's executive assistant. Marilyn has very honest eyes and a nurturing way about her. She also exudes a confident strength of will which I admire. She spoke to me slowly and clearly and was exceedingly kind all day. It does not surprise me Dr. Braddock hired such a lovely person to assist him.

Marilyn led me to a conference room where various Human Resources staff presented policies and procedures. They had me sign many documents. Then they played a security video. I am glad it was closed captioned because it was quite comprehensive. They take security very seriously here. As the video concluded, Marilyn returned. She smiled warmly and said it was time to introduce me to the entire department. That was the only time all day I felt nervous, walking with Marilyn to the break room.

Dr. Braddock was there talking with a few people. He saw me and smiled in his genuine way. I was glad to see him again. Standing near him calmed my nerves. As the room quickly filled up I looked at Dr. Braddock. His eyes were waiting. There must have been apprehension in my face because he said "These are good people, Bee. I chose each of them as I have chosen you." Then he turned to the crowd and addressed them. It was difficult reading his lips because his glance was sweeping back and forth across the crowd. I so dislike it when many people look at me at once, but I forced myself to meet their eyes. Most faces were mildly interested, some skeptical, some bored, some cheerfully curious. But there was one that drew my gaze and held it. He was a young man, tall, with dark hair. He was looking at me with an expression of sincere but confused recognition. And at once I felt the same. There was connection between us, a real yet blurred and distorted sense of ancient kinship. I do not know what or how or why.

Following my introduction in the break room, Marilyn and two other women, Deanne and Rosalyn, led me to my cubical and helped me settle in. Then Deanne and Rosalyn took me out to lunch. It was kind of them and they were polite to me the entire time but they did not always consider there was a lip reader amongst them.

After we returned I found a note on my desk from Dr. Braddock. He asked me to join him in his office at 2 p.m. I organized my cubical until that time then went to see him as instructed. There talking to Dr. Braddock was the young man from the break room. Dr. Braddock introduced him as Joe Graham. I shook his hand and our eyes met and again there was that strange recognition. I am certain he felt it too because his brow furrowed a bit and he blinked quickly and swallowed awkwardly. Dr. Braddock explained he was assigning Joe to be my mentor so that I would have someone to help me get accustomed to working at B.S.I. As Dr. Braddock spoke I sensed Joe studying me. When our eyes met again he smiled cordially and bowed his head respectfully. Then Joe looked to Dr. Braddock and I watched the two men speak to each other. There was meaning in their words but not nearly as much as in their posture and movements and expressions. And then I remembered Dr. Braddock mentioning Joe during my interview months before. This was the young man to whom Dr. Braddock would entrust his life. This was the young man Dr. Braddock loved as a son.

I returned to my cubicle and spent a while looking through various files and spreadsheets on the computer. One file was particularly sophisticated and I struggled to understand its utility. I wondered if Joe might help me. By chance his office is just across from my cubicle. The door was slightly ajar and I peeked through the opening. Joe was square to his desk. His hands were perched ready on the keyboard, though he was not looking at the document on the screen in front of him. He was gazing out the large window instead, out into the trees. He was thinking.

I knocked softly and Joe swiveled around in his chair. He smiled and stood up respectfully. He seemed happy to see me, or relieved to. I described the spreadsheet that was troubling me, the "RMM" file. He said he knew of it, that it had been created by a friend of his, a gentleman who no longer worked there. Joe offered to walk me through it and I said I would be grateful. I went back to my cubicle and waited for him to join me. While waiting I could think of nothing but the strange familiarity of his face.

A few minutes later Joe rolled a chair into my cubicle and sat down to my left. We stared at each other for several seconds then I pointed to the screen and asked him to share what he knew. He said that "RMM" stands for Reestablishment Macroeconomic Modeler. He said that when Dr. Braddock developed the concept of Reestablishment he thought it would be useful for nations to model and study interplay between independent and dependent macroeconomic variables as they relate to various treaties, trade agreements, and so on. He said Dr. Braddock figured, for example, that Canada might want to model the true economic impact of re-entering NAFTA given trends in timber futures. Or that Switzerland might want to study the value of re-endorsing an international banking treaty given fluctuations in the Prime Rate and LIBOR, or given changes in the relative strengths of the Euro, ruble, and dollar and so on. As Joe spoke, I appreciated the great duality of his face. It is burdened, taxed, like that of an old man, and yet it is naïve, innocent, like that of a little boy. It is handsome yet haunted. It is strong yet sad. It is complexly strained, yet sincerely curious. His eyes are an entrancing bluish green. As I looked into his, he struggled not to look away from mine. I am glad he made it so easy to read his lips.

I asked him to show me how the program works. He agreed and slid his chair forward toward the desk, closer to me. Then I saw the thick horizontal scar on his right ear. I could not help myself and I do not know why but I reached over and touched it. Then I traced it with my fingertip. I do not know why. I saw goose bumps on his neck and he shuddered. I lifted my finger away. He closed his eyes for a moment. When he opened them I asked how he injured his ear. He did not answer right away. I worried I should not have touched his ear. But then he answered. He looked at me and said he injured it on a farm. I asked excitedly if he had grown up on a farm but he said no, that his wife had. He said the injury was from an accident that occurred while he was dating her. Only then did I think to look at his left hand. There is indeed a ring there.

I asked him if the accident affected his hearing at all. He said no. Then I told him both my ears were broken, but broken on the inside. He asked how I lost my hearing and I told him about the illness, about the fever. I told him I almost died. He asked me how old I was when it happened. Nine, I told him. He looked down at the floor and I saw his face grow sad. Then he looked at me and said "My dad died when I was nine."

We looked at each other for a while. Neither of us spoke.

Then I said "We are alike then, Joe." I told him we each lost part of ourselves when we were nine. Then I told him what Grandpa once told me, that it was a damn shame me going deaf at that age, that any younger and I would not have remembered what hearing was like, that it would not have had any meaning to me so I would not have missed it, and any older and I would have had a grownup's perspective to help me cope, to help me mourn and grieve, to help me accept my fate and move on. I told Joe that Grandpa was right, that a nine year old has a tacky heart, tacky like wet concrete. It is a bit too old, a bit too hard to trowel over and smooth and make like new. And yet it will never completely set either. A deep impression at that age, a deep scar, never really cures. It never heals.

With very sad eyes Joe looked at me. Then without a word he stood and returned to his office and closed the door. I sat motionless at my desk, devoid of thought. I closed my eyes. I cannot say how much time passed but then I heard him. I heard his voice! With my ears I heard this! I heard his voice ask "Why?"

It is the same, the same voice that said "twenty seven" at the church of trees! My ears opened once again! With my ears I heard it! They opened at his voice. "Why?" he asked. He is the voice!

# 34

July 2, 2022

Geoff:

Yesterday I cleaned myself up and rode to my son's place so I could watch your press conference on TV. You looked so good up there, you old fox. I truly enjoyed seeing your face again, I really did. I laughed out loud and for a good long while at seeing how much grayer you've gotten. Your face, your expressions, those looks of confidence and doubt and victory and wonder. Then I got all weepy. I couldn't even talk. My grandson Matthew was mortified at seeing the old patriarch choked up and dripping big fat crocodile tears. I reassured him I was fine, but I really rattled him, the poor kid. I just couldn't help it. The memories all came flooding back, of when my life mattered, when people depended on me. When you used to depend on me. And now seeing you up there, so damn impressive and brilliant and seasoned and complete, it just busted me apart, and filled me up, like one seeing his child have a child, or noticing great wear on the spine of a book he's written. We teach men how to design and build things, how to survive in the wild, how to kill other men, how to love, how to father, how to sell, how to steal. But in all of history I don't think any man's ever been taught what to do in the wretched gap between the end of his meaning and his death. God dammit what could matter more than that?

Before I left, Ben printed me the latest draft of the G.A.C. Constitution. What a bloody mess. I appreciate that liberals view government as the ideal arbiter of social justice and provider of basic needs, but the document will no doubt enshrine a nanny state if that great litany of "…government shall ensure…" clauses remains. A constitution explicitly stipulating a "reasonable" minimum living wage, a "comfortable" retirement pension, "fair" provision for the infirm or disabled, and nationalized education and healthcare for all will certainly require structuralized wealth redistribution significant enough to make Marx blush. It didn't surprise me, then, to see the article on taxation. Does the phrase "…shall have the power to collect taxes on a person's or a corporation's worth…" mean taxation based on net worth? As in taxing wealth by debiting the net value of one's entire sum of possessions, holdings, and investments? I cannot imagine a more complex, onerous, and punitive system for a government to raise revenue.

Conspicuously absent is any right to keep and bear arms. I safely assume that is no oversight.

"The environment and any resources therefrom derived" are granted expressed legal standing? I shake my head at the imagery of some old woodsman in Michigan being sued by his maple trees, or some lobsterman in Maine being deposed by lawyers representing the crustaceans he routinely kidnaps and murders.

I see that Congress shall make no law abridging the freedom of "non-offensive" speech. Regretfully that's too little license for a man like me.

I'm tickled most by the article precisely reversing the tenth amendment to the U.S. Constitution. In the G.A.C. draft, "The powers not delegated to the states by the Constitution are reserved to the Great American Commonwealth." And so there shall be no federalism, and eventually no states, in the G.A.C. I assure you that will be the result – the immediate impotence and ultimate dissolution of each state in the commonwealth.

It's a good sign Bee hasn't written to me since starting with you. I trust she's been a good employee thus far. Make sure she's mixing with folks. She's sometimes too much like her grandpa, content to hide while stewing inside.

I'll ride into town later and vote, but it won't matter. Both sides think they've found utopia. Both sides are wrong. They'll realize it eventually. Uniformity of thought eventually requires oppression.

Bart

# 35

October 29, 2022

Just returned from a Halloween party hosted by Joe and Theresa at their home in Forthright. The whole department was there, along with their families. I purposely waited an hour after it started before walking over. Theirs is a charming 1950's neighborhood. The house sits well off the street on the outer radius of a ninety degree curve. It is a one story ranch sided in coppery brick and bright white trim. A proud fieldstone chimney pierces the roof. The shrubs are pruned neatly and the lawn is precisely edged. It had been freshly raked. The lot fans out like a pie slice so that the backyard is broad. There are many trees throughout the property, now all ripe with color. We both chose to live in Forthright, and just a mile apart. Not chance. Another sign.

Theresa was dressed as Dorothy from the Wizard of Oz. Her costume was very well done, every detail considered. Even with the makeup I recognized her immediately. I have studied that picture on his desk. She is tall and sleek. Her hands are slender and feminine. Her face is beautiful. Her nose is long and straight, a good match for her strong brow. Her eyes are deep set and protected by long curving lashes. She carries herself with grace and dignity, but without a trace of arrogance or pretention. As she welcomed me she was thoughtful with her pronunciations. She spoke slowly and clearly. She did her best to hide it but there was no mistaking the recognition. I saw it in her eyes, the same awareness of latent connection. She knew me somehow. And I, somehow, knew her. We both felt it, and we both just stared at each other for a long while. Eventually her gaze was broken and she stepped away.

Joe was dressed as the Scarecrow. He seemed determined to avoid me. After nightfall, though, I felt his eyes upon me as I stood alone by a torch at the split rail fence. I looked away from the light and into the dark of the trees and closed my eyes. As each time before, I wiped my mind clean of thought and waited. And then I heard his voice. "A cat." I smiled. I smile now recalling it. I kept my eyes closed, waiting for something more, but no. Then I opened my eyes. As my smile faded I saw a flicker in the dark of the trees. The glint of metal. I stepped over the fence rail and into the brush. From the lowest branch of a maple danced wind chimes. There were the seven brass tubes on the bottom, and above them the spinning disk of silver. And on the disk the angel, her wings to each side, her elegant hands pressed together in prayer held up against her face. Her eyes were closed but they betrayed her.

# 36

Colorado Springs is beautiful, our resort especially. The mountains to the west are so different from the Appalachians, but breathtaking just the same. We flew out on Monday. Dr. Braddock arranged this retreat in order to rally the department. He wanted to reaffirm priorities and objectives in advance of Expiration. There is just over a year remaining before this organization dissolves. I commend him for being so devoted to us, our unity, and our effectiveness. We have spent the last few days teambuilding. I have enjoyed myself immensely while driving cattle, whitewater rafting, and on the ropes course. Dr. Braddock came over and sat next to me at the bonfire last night. He brought a lantern with him. He knew I needed the light to see him speak. He is such a gentleman. He said with joy in his face that he has never seen me smiling so much, suggesting, I think, that I do not smile enough otherwise. I told him I am at home outdoors, under trees, atop a horse, and with wind in my hair. I told him these things remind me of home, of Mother and Father and the boys, and of Grandpa. He nodded and there was great meaning in his expression. He does not need to speak to convey meaning, and I do not need to hear to receive it.

I had resolved not to bring this diary along because I knew it would be a temptation. Now, though, I am glad I yielded. Today at lunch I saw heads all turn in the same direction. Marilyn was walking toward my table carrying a large white cake with candles burning on top. I started to fret, not sure how to react. But she set it down in front of Joe. The number 30 was drawn in green frosting. He blushed very brightly. As everyone sang to him I closed my eyes tightly and waited, but he thought nothing, nothing I could hear. All the things we share, all we have in common, and the same birthday, too. I do not understand it, this connection, as if we are cut from the same cloth.

This evening I noticed him leave the lodge. I watched, careful not to be seen, as he put on his jacket and headed down the sloping path, away from the resort and toward the stream and the mountain beyond. Somehow I knew he would be climbing tonight. I sensed his conflict and his desire to be alone, truly alone. He is so tortured, still tortured by the loss of his father. It is not a clean sorrow. There is anger too, some stain of injustice. I checked the time as he disappeared into the trees, 8:01 p.m. I went to my room, put on my coat, and sat out on the balcony. It overlooks the mountain and the path on which he will return. At 9:30 p.m. I began listening, eyes closed and mind clear. Time went by and then I felt it, I was there – knife blade cold, a rocky clearing, pines covered in ice, moonlight dancing off the crystals, a cathedral of diamonds, sparkling for him. A moment's peace, holy

117

solitude, creation's gift to this deep-bruised soul. Then motion nearby, clumsy footwork on gravel, an old man, short, shifting, struggling for balance. Connection of eyes, two statues, fear, excitement. Desperate thirst for purpose. Appraisal. Faith in omniscience, judgment. Worthy, immature, unripe. Frustration, but a morsel. Hope. Sour hope. Hope. A parting of the ways. Dark silence. I opened my eyes. 11:45 p.m.

# 37

May 26, 2023

Dear Grandpa:

Please forgive the decreased frequency of my letters. Do not interpret their sporadic nature as diminished affection for you, for your place in my heart has never been more secure. My excuse is the intensity of work at Bisection Inc. This first year certainly has been a change from graduate school – the pace, the stakes, and the magnitude of expectations. Regardless, I am guilty of neglecting not only you, but the sacred bond we share. I am sorry.

The significance of our endeavors at B.S.I. strikes me daily. We are methodically, peacefully, and completely dissolving what is arguably the most extraordinary nation-state in human history while simultaneously germinating two entirely new, ideologically-opposite nations to take its place. Our charge is surreal in every respect. The realization that it was my very own grandfather who inspired this odyssey fills me with both pride and a sense of utmost responsibility for seeing it through. There is a plaque hanging outside Dr. Braddock's office which reads "It is freedom that must survive." Those are your words, Grandpa. They, and so you, are changing the world.

Dr. Braddock is in fact all the good you said he would be. I have yet to discover in him a substantive defect, although I have been fortunate enough to meet his wife Beth on two occasions and she assures me he has plenty. There, too, you are correct. Mrs. Braddock is indeed wonderful. She is thoughtful, funny, caring, and wise.

My coworkers are generally impressive with respect to their professional credentials. All are well-educated, most articulate, and a few downright brilliant. They seem sincerely focused on executing their various assignments. I have not made many friends, however. You implored me to live fully, Grandpa, and I am trying, but I am so unlike the rest. Sound matters here, and most sound is noise, and noise is the most commodity medium of gossip, pettiness, and jealousy. All are repellants. All are prevalent in this place.

There is one here, one to whom I am drawn, one with whom I share a peculiar connection. I do not yet understand it and so cannot yet explain it. I am determined to find meaning in due course.

I love you, Grandpa.

Bee

# 38

June 16, 2023

It is a warm, sunny, breezy Friday, now late afternoon. The building is mostly empty, many took vacation today. I am writing from my desk. He is just across the hall. After lunch he asked if I would join him in his office to help him with a speech he is preparing for Dr. Braddock to present ahead of next month's national referendum. It was just an excuse to be with me. I am writing this here and now because I do not want to forget. I was able to hear him without closing my eyes, like the very first time, at the church of trees. It was amazing to see his lips moving, forming other words, words meaningless to him, while his mind emitted a separate stream. I struggled not to smile.

So small, petite. Expression melancholy, almost a frown, gravely serious, pouty. A doll's face. Gently curved, rounded edges, a sculpture of beach sand smoothed by hand. Skin fair, slightly golden, buttery, probably silky, soft. Narrow little nose. On its bridge three tiny freckles, similar sized and perfectly equidistant, with the third very slightly off-line from the other two, Orion's belt. Large eyes, green, like young grass, sad, like a puppy's. Long hair, rich strawberry.

# 39

July 1, 2023

Geoff:

You're such a faithful man, writing to me when I don't write back. I checked my notes and realized it's been a year since I last sent you a letter. You probably won't have to wait that long again. I think I've got my ticket out of here. Last month the boys confronted me about my fainting spells and labored breathing. I told them sternly I'd shoot them if they came out to the cabin, especially if they brought a doctor. They braved it anyway. Peter banged on the door and shouted that he was there with his brothers and daddy and a doctor and that if I murdered any one of them I'd burn in hell forever and never see Ruth again. I laughed so hard I nearly wet myself, though that's not a high bar at this age. The doctor was a very nice young lady. The boys stood there nervously while she examined me. She eventually said I have a heart valve problem, that it's serious, that there's a lot of leakage, that more tests are needed, that surgery is necessary, but she knew from my expression there'll be none of that. The boys knew it too. My son Ben went out onto the porch so the boys wouldn't see him. Philip, Jonathan, and Matthew just stood there motionless in front of me with looks of disbelief on their faces. And Peter cried. Big strong Peter. I told them one thing was more important than anything else, that they must not tell Bee, not yet. They all nodded, but Peter asked why. I said because the Songbird must not stop singing. Peter said "I understand, Grandpa." They sent Matthew back out to me the next day with some medicine. They know that besides Bee he is next most likely to weaken my resolve. I took the medicine from him and hugged him and told him I loved him. He is a smart boy and knew that from here on out I will not be swallowing any pills. That is why there were tears in his eyes. He told me he loved me and he left. They're such good boys, each very different, yet each his own reflection of the maker.

I hope to ride into town this afternoon to vote in the last referendum. Riding is easier than walking. It's still not simple, though. I'm so glad Bee is under your watch, Geoff. I'm glad beyond description. I'm ready to die. I'm not afraid. My comfort is the knowledge of her safety. The Songbird must not stop singing.

Bart

# 40

Dear Bart:

I rarely struggle for words. I do now. I shall not dishonor you by proffering hope for your healing and prayers for your endurance, for those are my desires and their cultivation, therefore, a transgression in selfishness. Instead, I shall confirm that I see with perfect clarity how all your life's needs and wishes have boiled down to one. As last and most enduring testament to our friendship, I pledge to carry on protecting, nurturing, and empowering that singularity to which you cling with all your heart. I shall do so to the very best of my ability. I shall do so all the days of my life. I shall do so tirelessly, with fervor and devotion, as you would have done. And so your life shall transcend mine. And so our friendship shall be sustained.

When she is in deepest thought, or she is challenged, or thrilled, or frustrated, or excited, there is a reflection of you in her eyes. It is more than just their prominence, or their brightness, or their vital green, Bart. It is that energy inside them, behind them, that fire.

You see her as songbird. I see her as flame.

Eternally,

Geoff

# 41

July 14, 2023

This afternoon I saw him looking out his office window. I could tell he was listening to music. He often does this on Fridays. I knocked. He invited me in. I asked him what the song was called. He was surprised I knew he was listening to music. I smiled and he smiled. He enunciated carefully. He said "Romance for Violin Number Two, in F Major, by Ludwig Van Beethoven." I asked him to describe it. I truly wanted to know. He looked past me, over my shoulder, thinking for a while. Then he said "I am not sure how to describe it." I asked him if he chose the piece or if it was playing at random. He said "I chose it." I asked him why. He took a deep breath then said "I am not sure." I said please. He looked past me again, over my shoulder, thinking deeply. Then he said that Dr. Braddock once described the piece as a metaphor, a musical metaphor, for life. Joe saw my desire for explanation and said that once, while the piece had played, Dr. Braddock pointed out its cycles, its oscillations, its transitions, from happy to sad, anxious to restful, simple to complex, defeated to victorious. He had noted the solitary violin, the narrative voice, the human voice, transcending. Birth to death. Life. I looked down at the ground so he would not see me closing my eyes. I cleared my head and waited, wanting so badly to hear it. But there was no sound.

Before I left him I asked where they live, her family, where she is from. Windthorst, he said. Later I looked, searched very carefully, but I could find no Brauers listed there. I did not tell him.

# 42

August 2, 2023

Bee:

I'm certain Geoff Braddock will end up either Harrison Keith's vice president or a senior official (perhaps Secretary of State) in Keith's administration. Geoff's been masterful in his work at B.S.I. His reputation sparkles. He's respected across the political spectrum. And he's not even sixty. Last I knew he and Beth had one daughter (and two grandkids) in Dallas and the other daughter (and third grandkid) in Wichita. This all adds up to Geoff Braddock being a fixture in Independence, Kansas for a good long while. You've learned and prospered under Geoff's leadership, Bee. He's sure to soon ask key staff to join him out west and with all my heart I hope you'll go.

Your whole life you've communed with the undulating forest of Appalachia. You've grown strong climbing its boulders and honed courage besting its peaks. You've found safety beneath its canopy, perseverance in its fertility, and serenity in its ordered decay. But in body and mind alike you should leave the forest now and go west, west out into the plains. There you'll discover your purpose, your holiness. I promise. I promise you'll discover it there amidst the endless seas of green and gold.

Far far in the distance, along the razor-thin line between earth and sky. It is there, tethering heaven. There you'll discover it, I promise. The Songbird's song.

Grandpa

# 43

September 24, 2023

Today St. John's in Amelith. This is a church in the round. There are six sections of pews, all taper toward the front, a giant hexagon. Parishioners must see each other across the way as they look toward the altar in the center. It is an odd design, and yet beautiful. I suppose all facing a single direction makes it easy to forget one another, that we are not alone, that we are a body, a community. But I am alone. I am seated in a middle pew. It is late afternoon. The morning's services ended hours ago. It is peaceful here. I may stay until nightfall.

I did not intend to walk this far, to have this be my destination. I only meant to walk close enough to their house to see the For Sale sign, to see if it was true, and then write from a swing in the park. But when I actually saw the sign it was a knife in my heart. I could not return home. I had to keep walking. I know it is best for them to move to Independence. It is right and wise and logical. But selfishly I have hoped. I cannot even write it here in you, to you, my most trusted friend. My wish. It has been so wrong to nurture it, so childish of me.

A man has entered the sanctuary. He is mopping the tiled floor. He is dressed as a custodian. I do not believe he has seen me yet. His mouth is very active. It looks as if he is speaking, perhaps singing, very loudly.

The man is getting closer to me. He is disabled somehow. One foot turns in quite severely and his hips are misaligned, but he is still able to mop and dust and straighten things as he makes his way through the pews. He is poorly shaven and has dark messy hair. He appears to be in his late forties or early fifties. He is definitely singing loudly. I cannot read his lips from here. His countenance is joyful and contented. There is healing in just watching him work. I am glad I walked so far today.

He saw me, set down his mop, and came over. He smiled as he approached and I stood up. He said his name is Leo and he bowed and smiled even wider. He has very few teeth. He asked my name and I told him and he said "buzz buzz" and laughed. It was an undistorted laugh, the laugh of one entirely unconcerned with how a laugh looks, the laugh of one concerned only with letting it free. Then he asked "You fly?" and I said no. Then he asked "You sing?" and I was immediately overcome and sat down and closed my eyes and covered my face.

I have opened my eyes and he is two sections away, still working joyfully, still singing loudly. Occasionally he looks at me and smiles. There is a piece of paper next to me. He must have left it on the pew. The paper is old and dirty and wrinkled. I held it up for him to see and he stopped and bowed and pointed at me. Perhaps it is his song.

*Come down oh love divine,*
*Seek thou this soul of mine,*
*And visit it with thine own ardor glowing,*
*Oh comforter draw near,*
*Within my heart appear,*
*And kindle it thy holy flame bestowing.*

# 44

January 3, 2024

Seeing you at Christmas was such a blessing, Songbird. Your beauty and poised presence are extraordinary. From little girl to grown woman, I have witnessed the transformation. What a gift it's been. None greater. As proud of you as I am, I assure you Grandma is prouder.

Also extraordinary is the strength of your character. I smiled when you confronted me about my illness. I smiled because of that fire in your eyes, that intensity, that daring boldness. Don't be angry with your brothers or parents for holding the secret. I insisted they keep it from you. If you're angry at being the last to know, be angry with me. I wanted it so. I didn't want you burdened one moment longer than necessary, for you have been burdened enough.

Fifteen years ago we learned your deafness was permanent. I know you remember the day. I knelt down in front of the fireplace and tapped you three times above your heart, then I pressed my finger to your lips, then I squeezed your hands. Several times in the years that followed you asked me what I meant in doing those three things, if there is significance to them. I didn't answer you then, because I was living. I'll answer you now, because I am dying. Yes, there is significance in those three things. From the heart comes creation, the establishment of glory. With the hands redemption is won, living flesh and blood required. And through the lips flows salvation, the dissemination of grace. You found peace and hope in those three things back then. For me, peace and hope abide in them still.

Bee, affection is worthless without finality. Affinity has no traction on an endless road. Mortality is the sole source, the sole source, of urgent meaning in everything that matters.

There is no love without death.

In that, rejoice with me.

Grandpa

# 45

Grandpa:

I love your most recent letter as I love you – beyond the power of human telling. Trust I feel no burden in knowing of your illness, for I believe you are at peace. If you are at peace, I am at peace. And trust I feel no anger toward anyone at making me the last to know, because I was not. I knew before the rest. What most score as disability and deprivation, I count as blessing. Deafness has granted me perceptions into the broader majesties of creation, aspects and elements and tapestries of meaning inconceivable with a full slate of senses.

The evening of my eleventh birthday I ascended the oak tree in our backyard. I climbed the rope ladder and entered the clubhouse through the trapdoor. I stepped through the window and crawled far out along the thickest limb. I wished to be alone and suspected I might be followed so I nestled myself in a tangle of leafy branches. After a while I noticed you coming across the yard. I watched as you stood at the foot of the ladder, looking up and studying the tree. I knew the boys had asked you countless times to join them in the clubhouse when they were younger and that you had always said no. I was surprised, then, when you grabbed the rope ladder and started climbing. Immediately the ladder began swinging and twisting and spinning. Your face turned bright red with frustration as you struggled. I could see you cursing and I started laughing, laughing very hard. I am laughing now just remembering! I covered my mouth, afraid you would hear me, because I could not stop laughing. My stomach hurt I was laughing so hard. Finally you reached the trapdoor and made your way inside. I could not see into the clubhouse from where I was hidden. After several minutes I grew curious and crawled back down the thickest limb. I carefully peeked inside the window. I saw you writing my birthday letter, slowly and thoughtfully. I saw you pausing here and there to find the right words. You finished it and read it back to yourself. Then you folded up the paper and tucked it inside a little velvet pouch. You kissed the little pouch and set it on the table for me to discover. And then you smiled. And I knew that you loved me. And my joy was boundless. It is boundless still.

Oh Grandpa, in all the world there is nothing so beautiful as you.

Bee

# 46

April 23, 2024

Dear Bart:

It has taken the United States of America one hundred sixty two years to return to Antietam. The trigger is different, the remedy different, the moral the same – tragic immiscibility. At high noon on June 16th the Expiration ceremony shall commence from the exact center of a bridge spanning the Potomac River just west of Sharpsburg. The two presidents-elect – Mr. Keith from the West Virginia side and Ms. Bradley from the Maryland side – will be sworn-in while flags of their respective nations are raised behind them. Immediately following will come swearing-in ceremonies for legislators and judges in Washington D.C. and Independence, Kansas, thereby establishing F.A.S. and G.A.C. governments. What happens next? Only God knows.

Bee tells me you are fading and that it will not be long. You have done so much for me, Bart, meant so much to me. The scales can never be leveled, the debt never paid back. But please have mercy and grant me this one last request, these three simple things. When you wake on the other side, smile a little boy's smile. It will be easy, I promise. Next, laugh like you have found your lost dog and he is all covered in mud. That, too, will be easy, I assure you. Then, after you have gone and done all the important things, take a seat at the end of the long table, the one under the tree down by the lake. And I will join you there. And time will be defeated. And we will spend all of it we wish getting to know each other in the new way, savoring together the splendor of the place, laughing together at the answer to every riddle, and the secret behind every mystery.

I love you, dear friend. Here, there, then, now…

Forevermore,

Geoff

# 47

May 5, 2024

Geoff my last to you. Can't catch breath anymore. Like a warm heavy dog sleeping on my chest. Could be worse. Too weak to get down to mailbox so you won't read till after I'm dead. This on the pile of final things. Give Joe his father's letter but wait for bottom. It's in the gold envelope. Sealed with wax and that funny mark. Ask him what it means and watch his eyes.

Ruth died and I wanted to die alone. Now I know that's impossible and I'm so glad. This wall of faces is so beautiful. They're all so happy. Joy pure. Don't know them but they know me! So beautiful smiling! Never stop. Too weak to move far but I want to touch them. No appetite anymore but would love some lemon pie here at the end. To taste the sour and sweet and touch these faces is all I want.

Goodbye son I love you.

# 48

May 9, 2024

The product of three threes.

Songbird my soul is yours.

# 49

May 11, 2024

My 25th birthday, Joe's 31st. Tomorrow Grandpa will be buried at sunset. His gravesite is ready. This morning I watched men dig the hole. A clump of dirt fell away and revealed a bit of the stone box in which Grandma's coffin rests. Seeing it made me feel better, not worse. It is a comfort knowing their bodies will be so close. That was Grandpa's wish.

I do not know how I will feel during the funeral. The ultimate disintegration of Grandpa's flesh does not trouble me. All that troubles me is my failing to sing. I was his Songbird but failed to sing.

Tomorrow I will tell Dr. Braddock I must decline his offer. I have decided to stay here in the east after Expiration. That is best, because Joe loves her with all his heart. I will earn my PhD. But before school starts I will go west, into the plains, to find her origin, to find the meaning. It must be there, where she began.

Before they close the coffin I will place a pencil inside. Grandpa taught me to write. And so to live.

# 50

July 10, 2024

On a plane to Wichita. There I will rent a car and drive west to see if I can find her home. He thinks of it often and with great fondness, the farm with the long white fence and rose bushes. I am sure I will recognize it. I must see it. The answer must be there, at the origin.

Just pulled off the highway. A sign says "131 Spur" and points north. This is it. I am sure. I do not know what I will find along this road but I have never been so excited.

Several miles north of the highway now and I have stopped the car. I am writing from atop a fencepost on the side of the road. It is so still, wondrously and divinely still. The sky is brightest blue. It is midday and warm. There is not a person in sight, just fields of green, and cows. Several have sauntered over to me. Their lumbering manner is sweet. It conveys curiosity and friendliness. I hope they appreciate my smile. They have such pretty eyes and long lashes. Their eyes are knowing and calm and peaceful. There are vibrations in the ground each time they tear up grass. They seem to be enjoying this exchange — my writing and their relaxed chewing. I am tempted to leave the car here and continue north on foot even though I know neither the length of this journey nor its final destination. I so wish to prolong this. I do not want this story to end. Perhaps I will just drive very slowly.

Stopped again. 131 Spur has come to a "T" and there are no signs. Now what? I think I will go right since I can see the road in that direction soon bending back to the north.

I have parked the car and walked up to a hilltop cemetery. A stone marker at the road says it was established in 1886. This is a tall hill and without a single tree so it is surprising there is no breeze up here. This cemetery is stark but lovely just the same. They have not changed the flag yet. The stars and stripes still wave.

There is not a single gravestone with the name Brauer.

The view from this hilltop is endless in every direction. There is not a soul to be seen, nor any vehicle but mine.

To the north, far far in the distance, barely discernible but unmistakable, is a steeple. A needlepoint. Tethering blue to green. Grandpa knew.

In front of the church now. My heart is fluttering. There is no one in sight. There is a house next door to the south but it seems abandoned. I am sure the church will be unlocked. I believe the answer is inside.

I am writing from the front pew. This is the most beautiful

church I have ever seen. Sunlight streams through the stained glass. The space is cool, with a scent like air above a fast moving stream. It is as if this has been set aside just for me. I may never leave.

I notice now a little room in the back of the church, the southwest corner. I did not see it when I first entered.

In the room is the answer. I cannot stop weeping. I might have gone my whole life without knowing. I sit again in the front pew. I may stay here forever. I am singing, crying and singing.

There is a strong rush of hot air. The church doors have blown open. It is the funny little man

# ACKNOWLEDGMENTS

There would have been no Bee without the love and support of a special few.

My friend Tim Dove created the perfect book cover, patiently tolerating (and wisely ignoring) my incessant meddling along the way.

My Dad Ted and my Uncle Tom carefully edited the manuscript. More importantly, they have always served as inspiration by way of their stubborn integrity and humble perseverance.

My Mom Cathie taught the power of expression, the filling of hearts with words and lives with meaning.

My friend Nathan Ulrey drove me to closure by pushing, pulling, and downright dragging me across the finish line, freeing the Songbird from her cage.

My children endured the peaks and valleys of my writing, my swings from grumpy to giddy, with wise recognition this is all for them.

And my wife Nicole was, is, and evermore shall be the source of all beauty in my life.

T.A
in e
but
dee
lum
gro

Mr.
sub

Made in the USA
San Bernardino, CA
04 May 2019